INSTANT MIND POWER

Here is a programmed-learning course which shows you how to build a 'filing cabinet' memory, solve your problems, improve concentration, overcome worry and fear and sharpen your powers of observation.

By the same author
HOW TO DEVELOP A SUPER-POWER MEMORY

INSTANT MIND POWER

A Dynamic Self-Improvement Course

by
Harry Lorayne

A. THOMAS & COMPANY
Wellingborough, Northamptonshire

This Edition 1979
Second Impression 1980
Third Impression 1982

ISBN 0 85454 065 2

Printed and bound in Great Britain by
Biddles Ltd., Guildford

CONTENTS

IMPORTANT NOTE

Do not skip *any* of the items in the following courses, no matter how simple they may appear to you. If you are already familiar with some of the material, the brief review will still be of great value to you in preparing for more advanced things to follow.

HOW TO USE THIS PROGRAMMED MIND-POWER COURSE:

All the pages in this book look like this one. Instead of being divided into paragraphs, they are divided into eight horizontal boxes like this one. Each box is numbered. Each one contains one bit of information — no more — and a question for you to answer about that information. Now go on to the next box (marked A) beneath this one

A. You're on your way! By advancing to this box (or, as educators call it, "frame"), you've begun the course. All necessary directions will appear in each of these little boxes, or frames, from now on. Notice that each of these horizontal frames has THREE separate divisions. This division gives you the information, and asks you a question about it. Now, go on to the next frame below.	This division gives you the space you need to write your answer to that question.	This division gives you the correct answer — so you can check your own answer to see if it is right.
B. This large division of the frame will always contain information and a question. To work the course, simply do this: STEP 1: Cover the right-hand box with a blank sheet of paper. STEP 2: Write your answer to the question here ——→ STEP 3: Slide the paper down so the correct answer is exposed. STEP 4: Check your answer here ——————	Always write your answer in this box.	┌→ The correct answer will always be in this box.
C. Now you try one— Columbus discovered A................... in 1492. STEP 1: Write your answer here ——————→ STEP 2: Slide the blank sheet of paper down to expose the correct answer. STEP 3: Check your answer here——————		┌→ America
D. If your answer is correct, continue with the next frames. Whenever you write an incorrect answer, check back to find where you went wrong. In this way, you learn from your errors. You learn from your e.................... .	(Write your answer here.) *errors*	(Slide down the blank sheet of paper to see the correct answer here)↓ errors
E. Do not skip any frames, no matter how easy the material may seem. If you already know some of the material, the review will help you in preparing for more advanced sections. Do not skip any f.................... .	(Write your answer here.) *frames*	(Slide down the blank sheet of paper to see the correct answer here)↓ frames
F. IMPORTANT: Each time you reach the end of a page, turn over the page . . . cover up the correct-answer side of the next page with your blank sheet of paper . . . and go on and read and answer the next frame: It's as simple as that. You are now going to turn to the next p.................... . Now let's have Harry Lorayne take over on the next page.	*page*	page

COURSE 1: HOW TO BUILD A FILE-CABINET MEMORY

1. This programed-learning memory course has been put together in such a way as to take you along step by s___ .	*step*	step
2. You won't feel a thing as you start to improve your m___y immediately.	*memory*	memory
3. It is like a game. A game in which you always win! If I've done my job correctly, you will answer 98% of all the questions correctly. And you will be learning wonderful new techniques of m___y training with each correct answer.	*memory*	memory
4. Be sure to answer every question. All q_____s must be answered. Now let's begin:	*questions*	questions
5. Let me assure you that there is no such thing as a bad m___y.	*memory*	memory
6. There are only trained memories and untrained m_____s.	*memories*	memories
7. I will show you how to rem___er as you've never been able to r_____r before.	*Remember* *Remember*	remember remember
8. I don't care if you think you have the worst _____ in the world! It is simply untrained. Just answer all the questions in this programed learning course, and I'll tr___ your memory.	*memory* *train*	memory train
9. Let's start tr_____ your memory right now.	*training*	training

10. The basis of a tr_____ memory is <u>association</u>.	*training*	trained
11. Association, as pertaining to m___y, simply means the <u>connecting up</u> or <u>tying up</u> of two (or more) things to each other.	*memory*	memory
12. Anything you manage to r___r now is due to the fact that you have <u>subconsciously</u> ass_____d it to something else.	*remember* *associated*	remember associated
13. Anything you've <u>ever</u> re_____ed, you've remembered because you subconsciously ass___ed it to something you <u>already</u> knew or remembered.	*Remembered* *associated*	remembered associated
14. The problem is that the associations you had before were subconscious; you had no control over them. I will teach you to a_____e consciously.	*associate*	associate
15. Once you can do that, you'll have a tr__ed m___y for the rest of your life!	*trained* *memory*	trained memory
16. To sum up, then, you cannot remember anything if you do not a_____ it to something else.	*associate*	associate
17. The things you already remember will aid you in remembering new information by making <u>conscious</u> ass_____s.	*associations*	associations
18. How will the things you already r___r aid you in remembering new information? Simple! You will learn how to assoc_____ any new piece of information to something you already know or r_____r.	*Remember* *associate* *Remember*	remember associate remember

2

19. This idea has helped you all your life. Even in your early school years, you were taught some new and difficult things by conscious a_____s.	*association*	associations.
20. Do you still remember that the lines of the music staff are E, G, B, D, and F? These meaningless letters were made easier to r____r by thinking of the sentence, "Every Good Boy Does Fine."	*remember*	remember
21. This is an example of a conscious a_____n.	*association*	association
22. The letters E, G, B, D, and F were the new things to r____r. "Every Good Boy Does Fine" was something you already k___ and remembered.	*remember* *knew*	remember knew
23. The new thing—the thing you had to commit to memory was ass____ed to something you already k___.	*associated* *knew*	associated knew
24. "Never believe a lie." If you r____r that sentence, you'll never forget that "believe" is spelled with the i before the e.	*Remember*	remember
25. The word "lie" is smack in the middle of the word "believe." Everyone k___s how to spell "lie." This will help you to r____r how to spell the more difficult word "believe."	*knows* *remember*	knows remember
26. "Never believe a lie"—is an example of a conscious a_____n.	*association*	association
27. Most of you were taught to r____r that the outline of Italy was shaped like a boot.	*Remember*	remember

3

28. Most of you still can remember the shape of Italy. The shape of Italy was the new piece of information. The b__t was something you already k___ and remembered.	*boot* *knew*	boot knew
29. Connecting Italy with boot was a conscious a_____n.	*association*	association
30. Do you see how simple it all is? The same methods and ideas can be used to r_____r any new thing.	*Remember*	remember
31. A conscious a_____n to help you remember that "piece" is spelled with the i before the e could be the phrase: "A piece of pie."	*association*	association
32. These have been simple examples of c_____s associations.	*conscious*	conscious
33. My methods and systems of simple c_____s associations can be applied to remembering anything.	*conscious*	conscious
34. Now let's add another rule: "In order to remember any new piece of information, it must be associated in some ridiculous and/or illogical way to something you already know or r_____r."	*Remember*	remember
35. It is much easier to r_____r and picture ridiculous things than it is to remember or picture logical things.	*Remember*	remember
36. The ass_____ns I'll teach you will be based on ridiculous mental images or pic___es.	*associations* *pictures*	associations pictures

4

37. These images or pic___s will be illogical or rid_____.	*pictures* *ridiculous*	pictures ridiculous
38. It is easier to recall or see a pi___re of a baseball bat flying through the air and hitting a lamp than it is to see the bat merely lying near the lamp.	*picture*	picture
39. It is easier to recall or see a p___e of a ridiculous carpet made out of millions of newspapers than it is to see a newspaper simply lying on a carpet.	*picture*	picture
40. Therefore, it is easier to recall rid_____s associations than it is to recall logical a_____s.	*Ridiculous association*	ridiculous associations
THE LINK METHOD OF MEMORY 41. I want to show you right now how ri_____s associations will help you to remember a list of fifteen items backwards and forwards.	*Ridiculous*	ridiculous
42. I call this the Link method of m___y. Because you Link together each item you want to remember.	*memory*	memory
43. Although you'll agree that you never before could have re_____ed fifteen items after reading them only once, you'll be able to do it easily by using the L__k method of association.	*Remembered link*	remembered Link
44. Here are the fifteen items you're going to r___r: carpet, paper, bottle, bed, fish, chair, window, flower, cigarette, nail, typewriter, shoe, pen, donut and car.	*Remember*	remember
45. Let's make ridiculous mental pictures or ass_____ns of these fifteen items!	*associations*	associations

46. It is important to remember that you must actually try to see the ri_____s pictures in your mind's eye.	*ridiculous*	ridiculous
47. If you merely think the words, you will not r_____r them. You must SEE the pictures in your mind's eye, if only for a split second.	*remember.*	remember

48. Let's review the basic rules again. Associations are easier to remember if they are: (choose one answer)
    (a) beautiful
    (b) logical
    (c) ridiculous
    (d) vague
	(c)	(c) ridiculous

49. When you create an association, you must: (choose one)
    (a) write it down
    (b) paint the picture
    (c) think the words
    (d) see the picture in your mind.
	d	(d) see the picture in your mind.

50. Ready? We will assume you already know the first item, carpet. That is the thing you already r_____r.	*remember*	remember
51. The first item is c_____t.	*carpet*	carpet
52. The new piece of information you wish to r_____r is paper.	*Remember*	remember
53. The second item is p_____r.	*paper*	paper
54. Now let's make a ridiculous a_____n between carpet and paper!	*association*	association

55. For example: Picture your carpet at home made out of paper. See yourself walking on that paper c___t and feel the p___r in it crinkle under your foot. See this a_____n in your mind's eye!	*carpet* *paper* *association*	carpet paper association
56. Here you must not simply answer the questions. You must stop for a moment and actually see that a_____n.	*association*	association
57. You have just made a ridiculous association between carpet and ____.	*paper*	paper
58. The ____ is crinkly because it is made of paper.	*carpet*	carpet
59. You must see this a_____n or picture in your mind for a moment. Then stop thinking of it.	*association*	association
60. In the Link method, once you've seen the r_____s association in your mind, stop thinking of it and go to the next step.	*ridiculous*	ridiculous
61. Any picture or association you think of between the two items is okay, as long as it is a r_____s one.	*ridiculous*	ridiculous
62. You are to select the a_____n you think is the most r_____s and see just that one.	*association* *ridiculous*	association ridiculous
63. For the first experiment, I will suggest one or two ridiculous a_____ns for each pair of items. Please remember that you must actually try to see the picture. Make it a mental image.	*association*	associations

64. You have already associated ____ to paper. Now simply stop thinking about it and go on to the next association.	*carpet*	carpet
65. Now we'll assume that you already remember paper. The new piece of information you wish to remember is bottle. You must a____te bottle to paper.	*associate*	associate
66. Remember, this is called the L__k method because it is like a chain. You always a____te the present piece of information to the previous piece of information.	*link* *associate*	Link associate
67. All right. A ridiculous association between, or with, paper and bottle could be this: You might see yourself reading a gigantic bottle instead of a p__r.	*paper*	paper
68. Or, you might picture a b____ pouring paper from its mouth instead of liquid; or a bottle made of p____ instead of glass.	*bottle* *paper*	bottle paper
69. Pick the association you think is most r____s, and see it in your mind's eye.	*ridiculous*	ridiculous
70. You've just associated paper to ____.	*bottle*	bottle
71. You've actually seen a mental picture of ____ pouring from a bottle instead of liquid.	*paper*	paper
72. Remember; you must actually ____ the picture in your mind's eye.	*see*	see

8

73. Now that you already remember bottle, let's <u>a</u>____<u>e</u> the next item.	*associate*	associate
74. Bottle to bed: Do <u>not</u> picture a bottle lying on a bed. That is not r____s or illogical enough.	*ridiculous*	ridiculous
75. Make the association ridiculous! Why not see yourself sleeping in a gigantic bottle instead of a b__? Or, see yourself drinking from a bed instead of from a <u>b</u>____!	*bed* *bottle*	bed bottle
76. See the picture you think is most r____s in your mind's eye. See yourself sleeping in that <u>b</u>___<u>e</u>. Or see yourself drinking from that clean white <u>b</u>_<u>d</u>.	*Ridiculous* *bottle* *bed*	ridiculous bottle bed
77. You've just associated bottle to ____.	*bed*	bed
78. Since this is of utmost importance for all my memory systems, I must keep reminding you that you must actually____ the picture you select in your mind for at least a split second.	*See*	see
79. You have just <u>seen</u> the ridiculous association between <u>b</u>___<u>e</u> and <u>b</u>__.	*bottle* *bed*	bottle bed
80. The next new thing to be remembered is, fish. The thing you already remember is, bed. So we must <u>a</u>____<u>e</u> fish to bed.	*associate*	associate
81. See a gigantic f___sleeping in your bed. It's flopping all around. The <u>b</u>__ is getting all wet and slimy because of it.	*fish* *bed*	fish bed

9

82. Remember; you must see this ridiculous picture in your mind. A gigantic _____ is sleeping in your ____. See the picture.	*Fish bed*	fish bed
83. You've just associated bed to _____.	*fish*	fish
84. We now remember f___; and that will help us to r_____ the next item—chair.	*fish Remember*	fish remember
85. See yourself fishing and catching ch___s instead of fish.	*chairs*	chairs
86. Or, see a gigantic fish sitting in your favorite ____.	*chair*	chair
87. Have you selected and actually s__n one of these pictures? Do you see yourself reeling up a c___r out of the water? Or, do you see a f__h sitting in your favorite chair?	*seen chair fish*	seen chair fish
88. You have just associated fish to _____.	*chair*	chair
89. Now we want to remember window. We must a_____e window to chair.	*associate*	associate
90. You might see yourself sitting on a window pane (it gives you a pain) instead of a c___.	*chair*	chair

91. Or, you're violently throwing chairs through a closed w____. Glass is flying all over the place!	*window*	window
92. See the ridiculous association of the chair and w____ in your mind's eye. See the glass flying as you throw that c___r through that w____w.	*window chair window*	window chair window
93. You have just associated ____ to window.	*chair*	chair
94. I want to give you a few simple rules to help you make r____s associations. But before I do, let's review.	*Ridiculous*	ridiculous
95. Think of carpet. What does carpet make you think of? Your carpet was made of ____, and was crinkling under foot.	*paper*	paper
96. What does paper remind you of? Wasn't that a ridiculous picture of paper pouring from the mouth of a ____?	*bottle*	bottle
97. A gigantic bottle was sleeping on your ____.	*bed*	bed
98. Bed. What did you associate with your bed? Wasn't it getting all wet and slimy because a gigantic ____ was sleeping in it?	*fish*	fish
99. Ah yes; a fish! Do you remember fishing and catching ____s instead?	*chairs*	chairs

100. There's glass flying all around because you're violently throwing chairs through your _____ .		window
101. Fine! If all your a_____ns were ridiculous and if you actually saw them in your mind, you're with me so far. If you didn't r____r one or two, go back and strengthen that particular association.		associations remember
102. We've all been raised to think logically, not ridiculously, so it may take just a little practice to make your associations r_____s enough.		ridiculous
103. Here are four simple rules to help make r_____s pictures.		ridiculous
104. First; picture the item or items out of proportion. In other words, larger than life. One way to make your pictures ridiculous is to think of the items out of p____n.		proportion
105. I've used the word, "gigantic" quite often. This was to help you get the items out of p_____ .		proportion
106. Second; picture the items in action whenever possible. I suggested that you picture yourself throwing chairs through a window and to see the glass flying around. That's a___n.		action
107. If you make the a___n violent, all the better.		action
108. Third rule; exaggerate the amount of items. As you go on; you'll notice that I'll tell you to picture millions of an item; that's ex_____n.		exaggeration

109. Last and most applicable:- <u>Substitution</u>. Simply picture one item <u>instead</u> of another. I suggested that you picture yourself catching chairs <u>instead</u> of fish. That's sub_____ .		substitution
110. You'll see more examples of this as we go along. Whenever you picture one item <u>instead</u> of another, you're using s_____n.		substitution
111. The rules then, are:- Make the items larger than life, or out of pr_____n.		proportion
112. See the items moving and in violent a____n.		action
113. Picture millions instead of one item—use ex_____ .		exaggeration
114. See one item instead of another—use s_____n.		substitution
115. Although it isn't necessary for you to commit these four rules to memory, you should try to get one or more of them into your a_____ns.		associations
116. In my sample associations that follow, you will always find one or more of these aids for forming ridiculous pictures: (1) out of proportion, (2) a___n, (3) exaggeration, and (4) <u>sub</u>_____ .		action substitution
117. Now to continue with our Link Method: The last thing we remembered was window. The new thing is — flower. We must make a r_____s a_____n between window and flower.		ridiculous association

118. You might see windows growing in your garden _instead_ of flowers. If you actually see them growing, that's action; seeing the windows _instead_ of flowers is sub_____n.		substitution
119. Perhaps you'd rather see yourself opening a window and a _million_ flowers fly into your face. Millions of flowers is ex_____n. Hitting you in the face (and hurting you) is a___n,		exaggeration action
120. All right. Choose a ridiculous picture and actually see it in your mind's eye for a moment. That's window to f____.		flower
121. You've just associated w_____ to flower. Actually see the windows growing instead of_____s.		window flowers
122. You've associated window to _____ .		flower
123. The thing we now know and remember is flower. The new piece of information is, cigarette. You must make a r_____s a_____n between, or with, flower and cigarette.		ridiculous association
124. You might see yourself smoking a large flower instead of a c_____e. Or: gigantic cigarettes are growing in your garden instead of f____s.		cigarette flowers
125. Select the picture you think is most r_____ , and actually ____ it in your mind's eye. See the smoke coming out of the f_____r. Or, see the c_____es growing.		ridiculous see flower cigarettes
126. You've just associated flower to _____.		cigarette

127. Please remember to pause each time to actually ____ the picture in your mind. That is essential.		see
128. The new thing to remember is, nail. We already know and remember cigarette. So, make a ridiculous a_____n between cigarette and n__.		association nail
129. Pretty soon you'll find it quite simple to think of your own ridiculous a_____s.		associations
130. For cigarette and nail, it's easy to think of picturing yourself smoking a large nail instead of a c_____. Or, you're hammering cigarettes into a wall instead of n__s.		cigarette nails
131. Select one picture and be sure to pause before going on and actually _____ it in your mind's eye. See the smoke coming out of the n__l. Or see those c_____s being pounded into that wall.		see nail cigarettes
132. You've just associated cigarette to ____.		nail
133. In using this Link method of m_____y, do not think of all the previous items. Just work with the previous and the present items each time. Just the two items.		memory
134. You've just memorized nail. The new thing to remember is, typewriter. You must make a ridiculous _____ between nail and t_____r.		association typewriter
135. All the keys on your t_____ are nails and they're pricking your fingers as you type. Or, you're hammering a gigantic n__l through your typewriter and ruining it.		typewriter nail

15

136. Select the most ridiculous picture, or one you've thought of yourself, and actually ____ it in your mind's eye. Feel those keys on the typewriter turn into n__s and prick you. Or, see yourself pounding that nail through that t_____and ruining it.		see nails typewriter
137. You've just associated nail to _____.		typewriter
138. The next thing to remember is, shoe. Since we already know or remember typewriter, we must make a r_____ a _____ between typewriter and s__e.		ridiculous association shoe
139. You're walking along the street wearing typewriters on your feet instead of s__s. Or, you're typing on your t_____r with your shoes instead of your hands.		shoes typewriter
140. Whichever ridiculous picture you select, you must actually ___ it in your mind's eye for a moment. See your s___s hitting the keys of that typewriter. Or see those t_____s on your feet as you walk on the pavement.		see shoes typewriters
141. You have just associated typewriter and ____.		shoe
142. Since you already know shoe, this is now associated in a r_____s way to the next item, which is, pen.		ridiculous
143. You're writing with a shoe instead of a p__n. Or, your shoes have gigantic p___s on the front of them, and write on the sidewalks as you walk.		pen pens
144. Pick one picture, and pause before you continue, to actually ____ it in your mind. See that s__e writing words across that paper. Or see those p__s on your shoes leaving marks as you walk.		see shoe pens

16

145. If you've actually seen the picture, you've just associated shoe to ____.	pen
146. Now the new thing to remember is, donut. You already remember pen, so make a _____ association between pen and d__t.	ridiculous donut
147. You might see yourself writing on a donut with a p n. Or, you're eating a circular pen instead of a d__t, and it's getting ink all over your face.	pen donut
148. There are many different r_____s associations that can be made with each pair of items. For this pair, you might choose to see yourself writing on a crumbly donut with a leaky ____. Or, you're dunking a pen into your coffee instead of a donut.	ridiculous pen
149. Select the one picture you think is most _____ and actually ____ it in your mind's eye before you continue. See that p__n dunking into the coffee and getting ink all over itself. Or see that pen writing your name across the crumbly surface of that d___t.	ridiculous see pen donut
150. You have just associated pen to _____.	donut
151. The last new thing you want to remember is, car. You already remember donut, so make a ridiculous _____ between donut and c_r.	association car
152. A large donut is driving a c__. Or, you're driving a gigantic d_____ instead of a car.	car donut
153. Select one of these ridiculous pictures, pause and actually ____ it in your mind's eye. See yourself behind the steering wheel of a huge d___t. Or see a life-size doughnut driving your own c__.	see donut car

17

154. You've just associated donut to ___.		car
155. If you've answered every question and if you've actually seen all the r_____s pictures, you will have no trouble remembering all fifteen items in <u>sequence</u>.		ridiculous
156. Why not let me work all the way from carpet to car with you right now, and see how amazed you are at your new and wonderful m___y. Here we go:		memory
157. Carpet—you were walking on a carpet made of p___. It crinkled as you walked on it.		paper
158. Paper—paper was pouring from the mouth of a b_____ instead of liquid.		bottle
159. Bottle—you were sleeping in a gigantic bottle instead of a b__.		bed
160. Bed—a gigantic f___ was sleeping in your bed, making it all wet and slimy.		fish
161. Fish—you were fishing and catching c___s instead of fish. Or perhaps, a giant fish was sitting in your favorite c____.		chairs chair
162. Chair—you were throwing chairs violently through your w_____, causing glass to fly all over the place.		window

163. Window—windows were growing in your garden instead of f____s.		flowers
164. Flower—you were smoking a flower instead of a c_____.		cigarette
165. Cigarette—you were hammering cigarettes into your wall instead of n__s.		nails
166. Nail—you were hammering a gigantic nail through your _____. Or, your fingertips were being pricked because all the keys on your t_____ were nails.		typewriter typewriter
167. Typewriter—you were walking and wearing typewriters instead of s___s.		shoes
168. Shoe—you were writing with your shoe instead of a p__.		pen
169. Pen—you were eating a circular pen instead of a d____.		donut
170. Donut—finally, you were driving a gigantic donut instead of a c__.		car
171. Did you answer all the questions? If you did, you realize what you have done, don't you? You've re_____d fifteen items in sequence.		remembered

172. If you didn't remember them all, go back and strengthen that particular a_____n.		association
173. Now, why not try it on your own? Think of carpet; that should bring the next item to mind. Think of that next item and that should bring the n_t item to mind; and so on down to car. Try it on your own.		next
174. Have you tried it? Did you r____r all fifteen? I know you did! Now let's try it backwards. Simply think of car; that should make you think of d___.		remember donut
175. Think of donut; that should make you think of p__. And keep right on going.		pen
176. You'll find that you'll be able to r_____r all of these items backwards, in perfect sequence.		remember
177. Now, if you've recalled all these items forward and b_____d, why not try a different list of items.		backward
178. The amount of items is immaterial, so long as you make a r_____ association each time, and always s___ it in your mind's eye.		ridiculous see
179. Now you can show-off to your friends! Have a friend call and list anywhere from ten to twenty items. You show that you can r_____r them forwards and backwards.		remember
180. You'll find that you can retain any list memorized via the L____ method for as long as you desire.		Link

181. Your original ridiculous a_____s will bring each item to mind like a filing cabinet.		associations
182. You can also remember as many L__k chains as you wish. Each one will be a separate chain, and will not conflict with each other.		Link
183. You can only find this out for yourself by trying and using the L___ method of m____y.		Link memory

PRACTICAL USES FOR THE LINK METHOD

184. When you use the Link system to memorize information of importance to you, it guarantees that you will r_____r that information as long as you need to.		remember
185. Simply linking this information into ridiculous associations will <u>set</u> it in your mind. Once it's set, the original a_____ns may fade, but the facts will remain.		associations
186. This system—and all my systems—are <u>aids</u> to your true memory. They are means to an end. Once you've remembered anything via the systems, you'll retain them for as l__g as <u>you</u> desire.		long
187. The L____ method of memory is used to remember things in sequence. Lists of errands and appointments are things in sequence. A speech or article is really only some thoughts listed in a s_____e.		Link sequence
188. Later on, I will teach you to remember things out of s_____e, but right now, let me show you some practical uses for the L___ method.		sequence Link
189. Say you have the following errands to r_____r for one day. Wash the car; make a bank deposit; mail a letter; visit the dentist; retrieve an umbrella left at a friend's house; buy perfume for your wife; see the TV repairman; buy a hammer; purchase a book; repair your watch; and bring home a dozen eggs.		remember

190. Well, you have a busy day! Instead of making notes, why not remember all these e_____s using my L____ method of memory?		errands Link
191. Assuming you've listed these e_____s in the order you wish to do them, you can use the Link method to memorize them since you'll now have simply a list, or seq___e, of things to do.		errands sequence
192. All right! The first thing to do is get that car washed. Then you have to go to the bank. Make a ridiculous a_____n between car and bank.		association
193. You might see yourself driving right through the glass doors of your b__. Get the picture? See the guards fleeing from the c_r. Now go on.		bank car
194. You must mail a letter next. So see yourself depositing l____s instead of money, at your bank. See the puzzled expression on the teller's face as you hand him your bank book and the letters. Remember, always _____ the pictures in your mind.		letters see
195. Now you have to remember your dental appointment. Make a ridiculous a_____ of your dentist pulling letters out of your mouth instead of teeth. See him pulling. See the forceps pulling out of your mouth—a letter!		association
196. Now make a r_____ association between dentist and umbrella. For example: your dentist is working over you in the rain; he's holding an u_____ over his head.		ridiculous umbrella
197. Now just go right down the line, associating each errand with the one after it. If each a___n is ridiculous, and if you actually s__ the pictures in your mind, you'll have them committed to memory in no time.		association see
198. The way to do it in actual practice is to memorize your list of errands before you leave your home. Then do the first thing. When that's done, it will automatically bring the next e___d to mind!		errand

199. Try it once and see for yourself! I cannot stress enough the importance of making the associations as r_____, as possible, and the necessity of actually ____ing each association in your mind's eye.		ridiculous seeing
200. Now you have learned how to use my L____ system to memorize all your errands for the day. The next simplest and the most obvious application of this L___ system is for remembering shopping lists.		Link Link
201. If you're going to the supermarket and you don't want to worry about losing your written lists, simply L___ together all the items you wish to purchase.		Link
202. Another valuable application is memorizing speeches and articles. If you want to memorize a speech you have to deliver, or an article you're reading, the best way to do this is to remember it thought for t____t.		thought
203. Our better speakers do not memorize a speech word for word. Since it is assumed that they know the subject on which they're speaking, memorizing each t____t in sequence is all that's necessary.		thought
204. Each thought in a speech or article will have one main word or phrase which brings the entire t____t to mind. This word or phrase I'll call the Key Word.		thought
205. We can use the Link method to memorize these Key W___s because they will form a sequence. Anything in s____e can be remembered via the L___ method.		Words sequence Link
206. If you want to memorize your speech, do this: First write it all out. Now look at the first thought. It may be in two or three sentences, but pick out the one w___ or phrase which brings that thought to mind.		word
207. Any thought in any speech will have one word or phrase which will bring the entire th____t to mind.		thought

208. If you have a choice of words, pick the one which is easier to picture. A noun is usually best. Pick a Key Word which is easy to p____e.		picture
209. Now pick the K__ W___ for the next thought, and so on to the end of your speech.		Key Word
210. When you're through, you'll have a list of K__ W___s which will bring every thought in your speech to mind in its proper seq___.		Key Words sequence
211. Remember that in every thought in any speech or article there must be one w___ or phrase which will bring that thought to mind. These words are K__ W___s.		word Key Words
212. If you read your speech or article to get the 'gist' of it, then go through it to select your K__ W___s, you will have a list of words in sequence.		Key Words
213. A list of words in s_____ can be easily memorized via the Link system of memory.		sequence
214. So use the L___ system to memorize these Key ____s.		Link Words
215. For example: You may have to give a talk for the Parents-Teachers Association. All right; first write the speech and read it over to get the g__t of it.		gist
216. The s____ is to be about the crowded conditions of the classrooms; and about the teachers (methods and salaries, etc.); you have some ideas on fire-drills; then you want to talk about the condition of the school furniture, and so forth.		speech

217. Read the speech to make sure you have everything you want in it, and to get the g__t of it.		gist
218. Now select your Key ____. They might look something like this:- crowd, teacher, fire, furniture, etc. `		Words
219. Make a L___ of these Key ____s, as you've been taught. Now link them together with ridiculous a_____s.		Link Words associations
220. Remember to make each association r_____ or illogical. And — be sure to s___ each picture in your mind's eye for a moment.		ridiculous see
221. If you've Linked the Key Words, you're ready to deliver the speech. Think of the first item and say what you want about it. When you're finished with that first item, it will automatically brmg the next Key ____ or thought to mind.		Word
222. This system of m____y and those following are all aids to your true memory. Just trying them and using them will immediately start to train your m____y.		memory memory
223. Use the above system for r_____ing a speech or article and you'll find that eventually even the incidental words will fall into place.		remembering
224. The rule is:- R___r the main ideas and the incidentals will fall into place.		Remember
225. You see, you never really forget anything you've remembered. You just need reminding. My systems and methods will serve as the reminders or aids to m____y.		memory

226. For remembering speeches, use the system just taught you. L___ your Key ____s. This will help even so far as delivering your speech is concerned. You'll have more confidence because you know you remember the speech.		Link Words
227. Keep in mind that if you r____r the main th____ts of the speech, the incidentals, the ifs, ands and buts will fall into place.		remember thoughts
228. And the exact same system is used to r____r articles you read. Pick out the Key ____s for each thought.		remember Words
229. L___ the Key Words, and you've memorized the article thought for th____.		Link thought
230. Do you ever have to remember lyrics and scripts? Although it's usually necessary to memorize them word for word, the L____ method and Key ____s will be of great help.		Link Words
231. Use the L___ Method just as I've taught you to. Remember the main thoughts in sequence.		Link
232. You'll have to go over it more often to get it word for word, but knowing it thought for th____ first will make the chore that much easier.		thought
233. If you have trouble remembering your cues in a play, why not a____e the last word of the other actor's line to the first word of your line?		associate
234. Even if your cue tells you to perform an action instead of talking, you can still a____ it.		associate

26

235. Although you can r_____ anything in seq_____ with my L___ method, I'll give you only one more practical use for it now. More to come later on.		remember sequence Link
236. Many people have trouble re____ing jokes and anecdotes.		remembering
237. This happens most often when you hear a batch of jokes at one time. Well, the system of Key W___s comes in handy when used in conjunction with the L___ system.		Words Link
238. Simply select a K__ Word from the punch line. That's usually best. Or, whichever word or phrase brings the entire joke to mind for you.		Key
239. You may have heard a gag about say, watermelons; then one about the political situation; then one about girls; then about a book; etc. These, then, are your K____ Words.		Key
240. A_____e watermelon to politics; politics to girls; girls to book, and so on.		associate
241. Since you were originally interested enough to want to r____r the jokes, these Key Words are enough to bring them to mind.		remember
242. Interest is very important to m___y.		memory
243. It is difficult to remember anything that you're not interested in. My systems almost force you to be in____ed, without your realizing it.		interested

244. Next time you hear a batch of jokes or anecdotes, try this system. Simply L___ your Key Words. You'll be amazed at the results!		Link
245. Although it isn't usually necessary to r_____r jokes in sequence (unless you're a comedian), it's better to remember them in sequence than not at all!		remember
FINAL REVIEW OF THE LINK METHOD 246. Let's take a few moments to review the L___ system of m____y.		Link memory
247. The Link method teaches us to r_____r things in se_____.		remember sequence
248. To do this, we always make an ass____n between the previous and the present.		association
249. An association consists of making a r_____s picture between two items.		ridiculous
250. These ridiculous associations must actually be s____ in the mind's eye for a moment.		seen
251. If you do this correctly, you'll be able to r____r a list of as many items as you wish, both forwards and b_____s.		remember backwards
252. A list of errands and appointments can be memorized via the L___ method because they are simply items in s____e.		Link sequence

253. To remember a speech, you must pick one Key W___ to represent each th____.		Word thought
254. These K___ W___ s are then memorized via the Link system.		Key Words
255. You can remember articles in the same way you remember sp___s.		speeches
256. You can remember jokes and anecdotes if you take a Key _____ from each and then L_____ them.		Word Link
257. Up to now then, you've learned to remember anything in s___e via the L___ method of memory.		sequence Link
258. A Key Word is a word that is (a) easy to spell (b) going to bring an entire thought to mind (c) easily forgotten (d) a synonym for something you wish to remember.		(b) going to bring an entire thought to mind
259. Any main thought in a speech or article can be brought to mind by a (a) Key Word (b) peek at your notes (c) prompter (d) recording machine.		(a) Key Word
260. You can retain any list memorized with the Link system for as long as you like, because (a) you like the list (b) you'll keep it in your pocket (c) you'll be using it (d) you're getting paid to remember it.		(c) you'll be using it
261. After memorizing a list via the Link method, you have formed a _____ of all the items. (a) chain (b) club (c) painting (d) history		(a) chain

262. If you've answered all the questions correctly up to now, then you understand the uses and workings of the L___ method of memory.		Link
263. We'll be talking about it some more later on, but right now we come to the Peg Method of m___ y.		memory
264. The P___ method will teach you to remember things out of sequence. But more important, it will teach you to remember numbers of any kind.		Peg
265. I call it the P___ method because it will give you pegs upon which to hang anything you wish to remember.		Peg
266. Just as in the Link Method you associated one item to another, in the P___ method you will learn some pegs to which you can always a_____e anything you wish to remember.		Peg associate
267. Most important, you will learn how to r_____ numbers.		remember
268. Numbers are the most difficult things to remember. This is because n____s are completely abstract and intangible.		numbers
269. I will teach you, via the P___ method of memory, how to make n____s tangible and meaningful.		Peg numbers
270. The P___ method will teach you to count with objects (that can be pictured) instead of n____s.		Peg numbers

271. Before explaining how it works, you must learn a simple phonetic language. This ph___c language is based on the way words sound. It is the key to the P___ method.		phonetic Peg
272. No need for dismay! This ph___c language consists of only ten sounds.		phonetic
273. With the simple memory aids I'll give you, it won't take you more than a few minutes to learn this ph___c language.		phonetic
274. These will be the most worthwhile few minutes you've ever spent. Because the P___ method will teach you to remember n___s and anything in conjunction with n___s in a way you never dreamed possible.		Peg numbers numbers
275. The method is based on the fact that there are only ten digits in our numerical system and only ten basic consonant ph___c sounds in the English language.		phonetic
276. Remember, there are only t__ digits in our numerical system, and only t__ phonetic consonant sounds in our language.		ten ten
277. I will give you one ph___c sound to represent each of the digits: 1, 2, 3, 4, 5, 6, 7, 8, 9 and 0.		phonetic
278. The sound will always represent that number and the number will always represent that s___.		sound
279. I will give you a simple memory aid to help you r___r each one. Once you know them, you'll always remember them. Now let's start.		remember

280. The #1 has only one downstroke. The letter t has only one downstroke. So, let's let the letter t represent the n_____ 1.		number
281. The letter t has ____ downstroke. The #1 also has ____ downstroke. Therefore the #1 will always be represented by the letter t.		one one
282. 1 = __.		t
283. ___ = t.		1
284. Remember that we are interested in the <u>sound</u>, not the letter itself particularly. Only the sound it represents. We are interested in the s____ more than the letter itself.		sound
285. The letter d has the same phonetic sound as the letter t. D has the same p_____c sound as t.		phonetic
286. The letters t and d have the same phonetic s_____:		sound
287. From now on, whenever you hear the phonetic sound of t or__, you'll think of the #1.		d
288. Whenever you see or hear the #1, you'll think of the ph_____ sound __ or d.		phonetic t

289. 1 = __ or __. Now let's go on to the next number.		t d
290. There are <u>two</u> downstrokes in the typewritten letter n. So, the sound n will always represent the n____r 2.		number
291. 2 = __.		n
292. __ = n.		2
293. t = __.		1
294. d = __.		1
295. __ = t or d.		1
296. 2 = __.		n
297. __ = 2. Now let's go on.		n

298. There are <u>three</u> downstrokes in the typewritten letter m. So, let's let m represent the #__. Or, as another memory aid, an m tipped on its side (Ƨ) looks like the #3.		3
299. The sound of the letter m = __.		3
300. 3 = __.		m
301. __ = 3.		m
302. 2 = __.		n
303. __ = t or d.		1
304. 1 = __ or __.		t d
305. m = __.		3
306. 3 = __. Now let's go on.		m

307. The final sound in the word fouR is r. So, let's let the sound r always stand for the #4. Remember it is the s___d not the letter itself that we're interested in.		sound
308. 4 = __.		r
309. r = __.		4
310. m = __.		3
311. n = __.		2
312. t = __.		1
313. d = __.		1
314. r = __. Now let's go on.		4
315. The Roman Numeral for 50 is L. That will help you to r_____r that the sound L will always represent the #5, and vice versa.		remember

316. 5 = __ .		L
317. L = __ .		5
318. 4 = __ .		r
319. 3 = __ .		m
320. 2 = __ .		n
321. 1 = __or__.		t d
322. L = __ . Now let's go on.		5
323. The letter j turned around looks almost like a 6 (J = 6). So the sound of the letter j will always represent the n____r 6.		number
324. The phonetic s__d of the letter j is the same as sh, ch, soft g, etc. All these sounds are made with the lips, tongue and teeth in the same positions. They are all the same ph_____c sound.		sound phonetic

325. Sh, ch and soft g are the same phonetic s_____ as the letter___.		sound j
326. Just as d is the same phonetic sound as __.		t
327. j = __.		6
328. sh = __.		6
329. ch = __.		6
330. soft g = __.		6
331. 6 = _ , or _ , or ___ , or soft ___.		j sh ch g
332. __ = j.		6
333. __ = sh.		6

334. ___ = ch.		6
335. ___ = soft g.		6
336. 5 = ___.		L
337. ___ = r.		4
338. 3 = ___.		m
339. ___ = n.		2
340. 1 = ___ or ___.		t d
341. 6 = ___, or ___, or ___, or soft ___.		j sh ch g
342. ___ = j.		6

38

343. sh = __ .		6
344. ch = __ .		6
345. Soft g = __ .		6
346. The sound of sh, ch and soft g all represent the number __ . Now let's go on.		6
347. You can form the letter k with two sevens. One 7 right side up, and the other upside down—(7K). That will help you to remember that the sound of the letter k will always represent the #__, and vice versa.		7
348. Hard c and hard g are the same ph____c sounds as the letter k. They too, therefore, will represent the #7.		phonetic
349. k = __ .		7
350. Hard c = __ .		7
351. Hard g = __ .		7

352. 7 = __, or hard __, or hard __.		k c g
353. Hard c = __.		7
354. Hard g = __.		7
355. j = __.		6
356. L = __.		5
357. r = __.		4
358. m = __.		3
359. n = __.		2
360. t = __.		1

361. k = __ .		7
362. 6 = __ , or __ , or __ , or soft __ .		i sh ch g
363. 7 = __ , or hard __ , or hard __ . Now let's go on.		k c g
364. The number 8 is similar in appearance to the handwritten letter f (8 8). So, the sound f, v or ph will always represent the #8. V and ph are the same <u>ph</u> sound as f.		phonetic
365. f = __ .		8
366. v = __ .		8
367. ph = __ .		8
368. 8 = __ , or __ , or __ .		f v ph
369. v = __ .		8

370. 7 = __ , or hard __ , or hard __ .		k c g
371. 6 = __ , or__ , or __ , or soft__ .		j sh ch g
372. 5 = __ .		L
373. 4 = __ .		r
374. 3 = __ .		m
375. 2 = __ .		n
376. 1 = __ or __ .		t d
377. 8 = __ , or __ , or __ .		f v ph
378. ph = __ .		8

379. __ = f. Now let's go on.		8
380. If you turn the #9 around, it is a p. P and b are the same ph_____ sound. Therefore, the phonetic s_____ of p or b will always represent #9, and vice versa.		phonetic sound
381. p = __.		9
382. b = __.		9
383. 9 = __ or __.		p b
384. b = __.		9
385. f = __.		8
386. __ = k.		7
387. 6 = __, or __, or __, or soft __.		i sh ch g

43

388. __ = L.		5
389. 4 = __ .		r
390. __ = m.		3
391. 2 = __ .		n
392. __ = t or d.		1
393. p = __ .		9
394. 9 = __ or __ . Now let's finish up.		p b
395. The sound for zero will be s, z or soft c. The first s____d of the word zero is z. This will help you to remember that s, z, or soft c represents the digit __ .		sound 0
396. We'll use the letter s as the representative letter for 0, since it is the most commonly used. Just as j is representative of sh and ch for 6, and f is representative of v and ph for 8, and __ is representative of hard c and hard g for 7.		k

44

397. s = __ .		0
398. 0 = __ or z or soft __ .		s c
399. p = __ .		9
400. f __ .		8
401. k = __ .		7
402. j = __ .		6
403. L = __ .		5
404. r = __ .		4
405. m = __ .		3

45

406. n = __ .		2
407. t = __ .		1
408. s = __ .		0
409. 0 = __ or __ or soft __ .		s z c
410. The vowel sounds, and w, h, and y have no meaning in the P__g method. We are only interested in the ph____c consonant sounds.		Peg phonetic
411. I'm quite sure that you know them all by now. But here's a quick final review.	No answer required.	
412. r = __ .		4
413. __ = 7 (choose any one of the sounds).		k hard c hard g
414. d = __ .		1

46

415. Soft g = __ .		6
416. 8 = __ (choose any one of the sounds).		f v ph
417. __ = 6.		j ch sh soft g
418. 2 = __ .		n
419. b = __ .		9
420. __ = 5.		L
421. 0 = __ (choose any one of the sounds).		s z soft c
422. __ = 3.		m
423. 1 = __ (choose any one of the sounds).		t d

47

424. sh = __ .		6
425. __ = 9. (choose any one of the sounds.)		p b
426. v = __ .		8
427. Hard g = __ .		7
428. Now let's see how these ph___ c s___ s help you remember all numbers—large or small.		phonetic sounds
429. The c in the word, 'coat' would represent the number __ . But the c in the word 'cent' would represent the digit__ .		7 0
430. The word, 'coat' has only two consonant sounds. The hard c represents 7 and the t represents __ .		1
431. The word, 'coat' therefore, must represent a two digit number. That number, of course, must be __ .		71
432. The word, 'cent' has three consonant sounds. Soft c = 0, n = 2, and t = 1. The word 'cent' therefore can only stand for the __ .		021

48

433. The word, 'butter' has three consonant sounds. The double tt is only one sound. Therefore, the word 'butter' represents the three digit number 91_.		914
434. Do you see how any particular word must represent one number or one series of n____s only?		numbers
435. Remember that double consonants are one sound only. Double tt is 1, not 11. Double LL is 5, not 55. Double dd is __, not 11.		1
436. Silent consonants have no meaning in our phonetic alphabet. 'Knife' would represent 28, not 728 because the k is silent. 'Limb' would represent 53, and 'dumb' would represent __ .		13
437. You must practice these sounds until they become second nature to you. Make it a game. Whenever you see a number, an address, phone number, price, license plate, etc.—see if you can't break it down into s____s.		sounds
438. Whenever you see a word on a sign, see if you can translate the word into n____s.		numbers
439. For the time being, try these:- What numbers would these words represent:- climb butler chandelier hypnotize bookkeeper		753 9154 62154 9210 9794
440. The sounds for these numbers are: 4319 6278 9040 14605 3189		RMTP JNKF PSRS TRJSL MTFP
441. Do not continue until you're sure you know all the sounds of the ph_____ language in and out of order.		phonetic

442. Do not continue until you're sure you know which sounds stand for which n___s and which numbers stand for which s___s.		numbers sounds
443. Now that you know the phonetic alphabet, I want to teach you to form ten Peg Words. These words will be formed as already shown by utilizing the particular consonant s___s.		sounds
444. I will select words which are easy to picture or visualize. The word itself is not as important as the pic_____ it creates in your mind.		picture
445. The Peg Word for #1 must contain only one consonant s___d.		sound
446. That one consonant sound must be the one which represents the number __.		1
447. The word, TIE, will always represent #1. Tie has only one consonant s_____. That sound represents the #1.		sound
448. Therefore 'tie' can only stand for # __.		1
449. Tie = __.		1
450. 1 = the word __.		tie

50

451. Most of the Peg Words I give will immediately suggest a picture to you. For tie, picture a necktie. Where I feel aid is necessary, I'll suggest a pi___e for the word.		picture
452. For #2 we must use a word that has only one consonant, and that consonant must be the letter or sound of __ .		n
453. The word, NOAH, will always represent #2.	No answer required.	
454. Noah = __ .		2
455. 2 = the word ___ .		Noah
456. 1 = __ .		tie
457. Tie = __ .		1
458. Picture an old, white haired man on an ark for Noah. Remember, it's the p___e in your mind that's important.		picture
459. I'm sure you know now that the Peg Word for #3 must contain only one consonant _____ , and that consonant must be an m.		sound

460. The word, MA, will always represent *__ . Picture your mother for ma, of course.		3
461. Ma = __ .		3
462. 3 = __ .		ma
463. Noah = __ .		2
464. 2 = __ .		Noah
465. 1 = __ .		tie
466. tie = __ .		1
467. The Peg Word for *4 must be one of these: a) car b) rat c) rye d) new		c) rye
468. RYE will always represent *__ . Picture either a bottle of rye whiskey, or a loaf of rye bread for the word, rye.		4

469. 4 =__.		rye
470. Rye =__.		4
471. __ = 3		ma
472. 2 = _____.		Noah
473. Tie =__.		1
474. __ = rye		4
475. The Peg Word for #5 is LAW. Picture a policeman in uniform, because he represents the____.		Law
476. Law = ____		5
477. 5 =__.		law

478. 4 = ___ 3 = ___			rye ma
2 = ___ 1 = ___			Noah tie
5 = ___ law = ____			law 5
479. ma = ___ tie = ___			3 1
rye = ___ Noah = ___			4 2
law = ___ 5 = ___			5 law
480. Which of these words must represent the #6? a) juice b) shoe c) rain d) bow			b) shoe
481. shoe = ____			6
482. __ = shoe			6
483. Shoe must represent #6 because it has only one consonant s___d and that is the sound for #___ .			sound 6
484. 5 = ___ 4 = ___ 3 = ___			Law rye ma
485. _ = Noah _ = tie _ = shoe			2 1 6
486. COW will always represent #7. The only consonant sound in cow is hard c, which must represent #__ .			7

487. 7 = ___		cow
488. ___ = cow		7
489. 3 = ___ Noah = ___ 6 = ___		ma 2 shoe
490. rye = ___ 5 = ___ tie = ___		4 law 1
491. The Peg Word for #8 is IVY. Remember that f, v or ph are the same ph___c sound. Picture either poison ivy or ivy growing all over the side of a house.		phonetic
492. 8 = ___		ivy
493. ___ = ivy		8
494. Noah represents the number a) 1 b) 2 c) 3 d) 4		b) 2
495. The Peg Word for #4 is a) Noah b) law c) shoe d) rye		d) rye

55

496. ivy = __ 8 = ____		8 ivy
497. #9 is represented by the sound p or b. BEE will always represent #__.		9
498. Remember please that --- the same ph___c sounds represent the same numbers!		phonetic
499. 9 = ___		bee
500. __ = bee.		9
501. The word "baby" could not represent #9 because it has two consonant s___s.		sounds
502. The Peg Word, TIE, represents number a) 4 b) 6 c) 1 d) 7		c) 1
503. #8 is represented by the word, a) ivy b) bee c) rye d) law		a) ivy
504. Now, the Peg Word for #10 must contain two consonant s___s, because it has __ digits.		sounds two

505. Since t is the sound for one and s or z is the s___d for zero, we can use the word, TOES. The sounds, of course, are in the proper order.		sound
506. Why does the word for #10 have to have two consonant s___s? Because #10 has___digits.		sounds two
507. Toes = _		10
508. ___ = 10		toes
509. 1 = ___ 6 = ___ 2 = ___ 7 = ___ 3 = ___ 8 = ___ 4 = ___ 9 = ___ 5 = ___ 10 = ___		tie shoe Noah cow ma ivy rye bee law toes
510. _ = ivy __= Noah __ = rye __= law __ = tie __ = ma __ = cow __ = bee __ = toes __ = shoe		8 2 4 5 1 3 7 9 10 6
511. Most probably you already know all the P__ Words by simply having filled in the blanks up to now.		Peg
512. Your m___y is a fantastic machine. If at first, you're not sure of a Peg Word, all you have to know is the sound.		memory
513. Say you want the word for #1. You know the sound is t, but you can't think of the w__d itself.		word

514. Simply think of the sound and say any word that comes to mind containing that consonant _____ (or sounds) only. "Toy, tow, tea, tie."		sound
515. As soon as you say the right P___ Word, it will 'ring a bell' in your mind, and you'll know it. The Peg Word for #1 is ___.		Peg tie
516. So you see, it's the s___d that's of utmost importance.		sound
517. Thorough knowledge of the ten ph___c sounds will make it a simple task to make up your own Peg Words for numbers, as you'll see in a little while.		phonetic
NOW PUT YOUR NEW NUMBER-MEMORY TO WORK 518. Right now, let me show you how the ten P__ W___s can help you memorize ten objects in and <u>out</u> of order after hearing or seeing them only once.		Peg Words
519. The Pegs will always remain the same. Once you make them up and r_____r them, you'll <u>always</u> have these Pegs to hang new information onto.		remember
520. So be absolutely sure you know the first ten P__ W___s in and out of order before you continue.		Peg Words

521. Here are ten items numbered out of order, which you will r_____r in no time at all:
 	
  9. purse   5. key
  6. cigarette   2. TV set
  4. airplane   8. wrist watch
  (see next frame)
		remember

521. (continued)
 	
  7. salt-shaker   10. telephone
  3. lamp   1. glass
	No answer required.	

58

522. All you have to do to memorize these ten items in and out of order, is to ass____e the item to the <u>Peg Word</u> for its number!		associate
523. You have already learned how to make a___-____ns and how to make them r_____s.		associations ridiculous
524. You have also learned that you must actually s__ the ridiculous associations in your mind.		see
525. You'll be doing the same thing here; but instead of associating items to each other as in the Link method, you'll be associating the item to the P___Word.		Peg
526. All right. You have to remember that a purse is #9. The Peg Word for #9 is, bee. So make a ridiculous a _____ n between, or with, purse and bee.		association
527. You might see yourself opening a purse and a million (exaggeration) bees swarm out, stinging you (action). Be sure to s__ the picture in your mind's eye.		see
528. The item to remember for #6 is cigarette. The P__ Word for #6 is, shoe. See yourself smoking a shoe instead (substitution) of a cigarette. Or, you're wearing gigantic (out of proportion) cigarettes instead of shoes. Select one and <u>see</u> it in your mind for a moment.		Peg
529. You have, so far, associated bee to p____ , and shoe to c_____.		purse cigarette
530. #4 is, airplane. A r_____s association between plane and the Peg Word for #4 (rye) might be:- a gigantic loaf of rye bread is flying in the sky like an airplane. Pause for a moment and <u>see</u> the picture.		ridiculous

531. #7 is salt-shaker. The P___Word for #7 is, cow. See yourself milking a cow and salt-shakers are coming out instead of milk. Or, the cow has salt-shakers instead of udders! See the picture.		Peg
532. You have associated shoe to c _____ ; bee to p___ ; cow to s_____ ; and rye to a_____ .		cigarette purse salt-shaker airplane
533. #3 (ma) is, lamp. See your ma wearing a gigantic lamp. See the lamp going on and off. Remember to pause and s___the picture in your mind.		see
534. #5 (law) is, key. See a gigantic key swinging a club and walking the beat like a policeman. Remember to s___the picture.		see
535. #2 (Noah) is, TV set. You might see Noah sailing on a TV set instead of an ark. You must s__the picture in your mind's eye.		see

536. So far, you have associated
  purse and b____
  shoe to c____
  airplane and r____
  cow to s_____
		bee
		cigarette
		rye
		salt-shaker

537. And -
  ma to l_____
  key and l___
  Noah to T___
		lamp
		law
		TV

538. The item to remember for #8 (ivy) is, wrist watch. You can see millions of wrist watches growing all over the side of your house instead of ivy. Or, you're wearing ivy on your wrist instead of a watch. Select the one you think is most r_____ s and see it in your mind.		ridiculous
539. #10 (toes) is, telephone. You might see yourself dialing with your toes, or, you pick up the phone and it turns out you're holding your toes to your ear. Be sure to actually s_ the picture.		see

540. #1 (tie) is, glass. See yourself wearing a gigantic glass instead of a necktie. Or, you're drinking neckties from a glass; or, a large glass is wearing a necktie. Select one and s__ it in your mind.		see
541. You've associated ivy to w_____ ; toes to t _____ ; and tie to g___.		wristwatch telephone glass
542. If you've made all your associations r_____s enough and strong enough, you've just remembered ten items which were given to you completely out of order!		ridiculous
543. You've also r_____red them forwards, backwards and out of order. You don't believe it? Well, I'll prove it to you in a moment.		remembered
544. In the next frame or two, I'll have ten numbered blanks for you to fill in. If you do fill them all in, then you've r_____red the ten items.		remembered
545. An example of how to go about it: You want to remember the item for #1. The s___d for one is t. That makes you think of the Peg Word, t__.		sound tie
546. What does tie make you think of? Well, weren't you wearing a gigantic glass instead of a tie? Then the item for #1 is, ____.		glass
547. Fill in these blanks with the correct memorized items. 1. g____ 6. c_____ 2. t____ 7. s _____ (see next frame)		glass cigarette TV salt-shaker
547. (continued) 3. l____ 8. w ____ 4. a____ 9. p ____ 5. k____ 10. t _____		lamp wrist-watch airplane purse key telephone

61

548. Did you get them all? I'm sure you did. If you missed one or two, go back and strengthen that particular a _____ n.		association

549. Now try it out of order.		cigarette lamp
6. 3.		airplane wrist-watch
4. 8.		purse TV
9. 2.		
(see next frame)		

549. (continued)		
7. 5.		salt-shaker key
1. 10.		glass telephone

550. You realize that if you heard the item, you'd know which number it belonged to! The item would bring the P__ Word to mind.		Peg

551. Say you heard, airplane. Well, a loaf of rye bread was flying in the sky; or, you were eating a plane instead of bread. Rye is the P___Word for #4. So, airplane must be #__.		Peg 4

552. Now fill in these blanks with the proper numbers:-			
TV set key		2	5
lamp glass		3	1
telephone salt-shaker		10	7
(see next frame)			

552. (continued)			
purse cigarette		9	6
watch airplane		8	4

553. Finally try this:-		telephone key
10. _____ 5. _____		purse airplane
9. _____ 4. _____		wrist-watch lamp
8. _____ 3. _____		salt-shaker TV
7. _____ 2. _____		cigarette glass
6. _____ 1. _____		

554. Do you realize what you've accomplished? You've r_____red ten items given to you in a haphazard order and you've remembered them forwards, backwards and inside out!		remembered

555. Do you see how the ____ Words help you remember things out of order?		Peg
NOW MAKE YOUR MEMORY EVEN MORE POWERFUL 556. You should now be amazed at your own m____y power! But wait, why not remember twenty items instead of ten?		memory
557. I will help you to make up P__ Words up to #20. After that you can make them up by yourself. It's easy.		Peg
558. Since #11 has two digits, the _____ Word for it must have two consonant s____s. Each sound must be a t or d to represent the digit 1. The Peg for #11 is, TOT. Picture an infant.		Peg sounds
559. 11 = __.		tot
560. __ = tot.		11
561. The Peg Word for #12 must contain the s____s t and n in that order. Ton, tone, tan or tune would do. But it's easier to picture, TIN. So TIN will always represent #12.		sounds
562. 12 = __.		tin
563. __ = tin.		12

564. Tot = ___ ___ = 11		11 tot
Tin = ___ ___ = 12		12 tin
565. For #13 we'll use, TOMB. (Remember the b is silent.) Picture a gravestone. Do you see why tomb can only stand for #___?		13
566. Tomb = __.		13
567. ___ = 13.		tomb
568. Tot = ___		11
Tin = ___		12
Tomb = ___		13
569. The Peg Word for #14 is, TIRE. Tire = __.		14
570. 14 = ___		tire
571. 11 = ___		tot
12 = ___		tin
13 = ___		tomb
14 = ___		tire
572. The Peg Word for #15 is, TOWEL. Towel = __.		15

573. ____ = 15.		Towel
574. Tin = ____ Towel = ____ Tire = ____ Tot = ____ Tomb = ____		12 15 14 11 13
575. 14 = ____ 11 = ____ 13 = ____ 12 = ____ 15 = ____		tire tot tomb tin towel
576. The easiest Peg to picture for #16 is, DISH. d = 1, sh = 6. dish = ____		16
577. ____ = 16.		dish
578. Tin = __. 15 = ____. Tire = __.		12 towel 14
579. 11 = __. Tomb = __. 16 = ____,		tot 13 dish
580. For #17, we'll use, TACK. t = 1. ck is one sound, and it represents 7. Tack = __.		17
581. 17 = ____.		tack

582. 15 = _____ _____ = 13		towel tomb
12 = _____ _____ = 16		tin dish
17 = _____ _____ = 14		tack tire
11 = ___		tot

583. For #18, we need a t or d and a f or v sound in that order. The Peg Word for #18 is, DOVE. Dove = ___.

18

584. _____ = 18.

Dove

585. Dish = ___. Tack = ___.		16 17
Tomb = ___. Towel = ___.		13 15
Tot = ___. Tin = ___.		11 12
Dove = ___. Tire = ___.		18 14

586. The Peg Word for #19 is, TUB. Tub = ___.

19

587. 19 = ___.

  ___ = 19.

tub

Tub

588. There are two digits in the #20. The sounds for these digits are n and s or z in that order. So the Peg for #20 is, NOSE. Nose = ___.

20

589. 20 = _____.

nose

590. 11 = ___. 16 = _____.		tot dish
12 = ___. 17 = _____.		tin tack
13 = _____. 18 = _____.		tomb dove
14 = _____. 19 = ___.		tire tub
15 = _____. 20 = _____.		towel nose

		tub	tot
		tomb	tack
		tin	tire
		dove	dish
		nose	towel

591. Try them out of order:-

19 = ___ .   11 = ___.
13 = ___ .   17 = ___ .
12 = ___.   14 = ___ .
18 = ___ .   16 = ___ .
20 = ___ .   15 = ___ .

---

		tie	shoe
		Noah	cow
		ma	ivy
		rye	bee
		law	toes

592. Now see if you still know these:-

1 = ___ .   6 = ___ .
2 = ___ .   7 = ___ .
3 = ___ .   8 = ___ .
4 = ___ .   9 = ___ .
5 = ___ .   10 = ___ .

---

593. See how easy it is? It's not as if the **P**___ Words were just _any_ words. They must fit into the ph___c language, so they're easy to remember.

Peg

phonetic

---

594. After a little more practice, you should know them as well as you know the numbers. You should be able to recite them as quickly as you can count. Put in some practice learning these ___ Words.

Peg

---

595. Now, if you want to show off, have a friend number a paper from 1 to 20. Have him call out a number. Then have him call out a tangible object for that number. You ass___ e the object to the P___ Word for the number.

associate

Peg

---

596. After he's called them all, and written them so he'll remember them, you show that you r_____r them forwards, backwards and in and out of order.

remember

---

597. I'm sure you realize by now that you can create a P___ Word for _any_ number. For 900, you could use basis or _bases_. For 821 _fiend_; 1439 — tramp, etc.

Peg

---

598. This is not necessary, of course. If you know the _sounds_ of the ph___ alphabet, you can make up the words as _you_ need them.

phonetic

---

599. You can, if you like, make your own list up to 100. Although these can be made up as they're necessary, it might facilitate your m___y for numbers if you've got them ready, as you'll see later on. This is up to you.

memory

67

600. If you do want to make up the list now, keep in mind that the words must fit the ph____ language.		phonetic
601. Also, select only words that can easily be pictured. Nouns are best. It is what you actually s__ in your mind that helps you to re_____ r.		see remember
602. And finally, try not to select words which will create a similar picture, or conflict, with other words. For example — for 82, do not use, vine. This is too similar to the word for #8, which is ___. Phone would be better.		ivy
603. For 78, you could use CAVE; for 97 — BOOK; for 52 — LION; for 71 — COT; for 64 — CHERRY; for 46 — ROACH; for 29 — KNOB; for 39 — PICTURE; 100 — DISEASE, etc. Do you see how each _____ Word fits our ph_____ language?		Peg phonetic
604. The Peg system will help you to remember things in and ___ of order.		out
605. It is a simple matter to remember the Peg Words because each word must fit its number via the ph_____ language.		phonetic
606. Now I want to show you how to use what you've already learned of the P__ method for some other practical purposes.		Peg
607. First of all, you can use the P___method in place of, or in conjunction with, the Link method.		Peg
608. For things to be remembered in sequence only, the L __ system is best.		Link

609. However, if the exact sequence is not important, or even if it is and you want to know the information out of sequence, too — then the P___ system is the one to use.		Peg
610. For example: You can remember your errands and appointments with the P___system just as you memorized the ten items in and out of order.		Peg
611. Assume you had the same errands to take care of as when I taught you the L___method. Wash the car; bank deposit; mail a letter; dentist appointment; get umbrella; perfume for wife, etc.		Link
612. Simply a_____te car to tie; bank to Noah; letter to ma; dentist to rye; umbrella to law; perfume to shoe, and so on.		associate
613. The L___ method can be used in conjunction with this Peg system if at one of your stops you have to buy more than one item and you want to make sure you r_____r them.		Link remember
614. For example, one of your errands is to stop at a department store and buy a toaster, a hammer, a bulb, rubber bands and a bathroom scale. How would you r_____r all of them?		remember
615. If your trip to the store were #7, simply a___-___e department store to cow. Now L___ store to toaster; toaster to hammer; hammer to bulb; bulb to rubber bands and rubber bands to bathroom scale.		associate Link
616. That's all! Associate your next errand to #8 (ivy). The L___ will take care of the incidentals of each errand for you.		Link
617. Utilizing the P___ method, you can do your errands in any order you like. But it works just as well if you want to do them in s_____e.		Peg sequence

618. After memorizing the list with the P___method, think of, tie. That will remind you of your first errand or appointment.		Peg
619. When that chore is done, think of Noah. That will tell you what you must take care of next. Then think of __ , to remind you of the third errand, and so forth.		ma
620. Let's go on to other applications. Do you see how the P___ method is useful for remembering appointments? Simply associate the first appointment to tie; the second to Noah; and so on.		Peg
621. You can r_____ r the Key Words of your speech this way too. A_____e the first Key Word to tie; the second to Noah; and so on.		remember associate
622. If during one particular thought, you have to r_____r a series of lesser thoughts pertaining to the main thought, use the L___there.		remember Link
623. That will assure you that you do not forget <u>any</u> important parts of your sp____ .		speech
HOW TO REMEMBER PRICES AND STYLE NUMBERS 624. Let me repeat again — the most important thing you've ever learned is the ph___ alphabet.		phonetic
625. I said before that numbers are the most difficult things to r_____r. They are completely abstract and meaningless.		remember
626. You now have at your fingertips the key to making ALL n____rs, forevermore, meaningful, interesting and tangible.		numbers

627. Half the battle in r_____ing anything is to make intangibles tangible and meaningless information m_____ful.		remembering meaningful
628. In a little while, you'll be amazed at your new found ability to r_____r prices, style numbers, telephone numbers, addresses, long digit numbers — numbers of any kind.		remember
629. Actually, you have the ability and the knowledge for re_____ing numbers right now. I just have to show you how to apply the ph____ alphabet.		remembering phonetic
630. Assume that for some reason you have to r_____r that a certain toaster is priced at $18.11.		remember
631. Your Peg Word for 18 is, dove; the Peg W____for 11 is, tot. Associate toaster to dove and tot in <u>one</u> picture.		Word
632. For example, you might <u>see</u> doves flying out of a toaster instead of bread, and the doves are flying to, and pecking at, an infant (tot). You must s___ the picture in your mind's eye.		see
633. Once you've made this picture or a_____tion, you'll find it easy to remember that that toaster costs $18.11.		association
634. Every time you think of toaster, the r_____s picture of doves flying out of it and attacking a child will come to mind.		ridiculous
635. Simply revert or translate the Peg W___s (or sounds) back to numbers — and you have the price!		Words

636. If you have no definite P___Word for the numbers, it doesn't matter. Make up the words as you go along.		Peg
637. If you had to r _____ r that a TV set was priced at $142.95, you could make a picture of a <u>train</u> with a gigantic <u>bell</u> coming right out of the screen of a TV set.		remember
638. Train = 142; bell = 95. Do you see how it is the <u>sounds</u> that tell you the price? The s___ s are the important things.		sounds
639. Even for the original example: - A toaster at $18.11. One word could do the trick. Ass____e toaster to <u>tufted</u>. Tufted — 1811. It's fun to make up pictures like this.		Associate
640. If you've practiced the ph___ language as you should have, you'll be able to make up a word, or words, for any price. Or any number, for that matter.		phonetic
641. See if you can follow these:- $94.21 — brained; $14.54 — trailer; $158.62 — television; $920.50 — pencils; $97.15 — big towel or pigtail; $6_____ — checkers.		$67.40
642. Make up your words to cover as many digits as possible. If you need, or use, more than one word, simply make an ass___tion or picture which gets all the words in! Or, use the L___ if necessary.		association Link
643. Can you make up a word, or words, for these prices? 　　$941.00 b_____ 　　$ 23.94 n_____ 　　$ 51.40 l_____		bronzes number letters
644. The word, or words, for $940.51 could be, 　a) necklace 　b) sentence 　c) brighter 　d) bracelet		d) bracelet

72

645. Here is a list of items and their prices; see if you can r_____r them all. toaster - $18.11 dress - $ 42.50 steam iron - $19.85 chair - $112.34 (see next frame)		remember
645. (continued) radio - $28.72 book - $ 6.52 lighter - $10.15 lamp - $ 14.61	No answer required.	
646. If you made up words for each price and made a strong ridiculous a_____n between the words and the item, you should remember them all.		association

647. See if you do:-
 	
        toaster _____   dress _____
        steam iron _____   chair _____
        radio _____   book _____
        lighter _____   lamp _____
		$18.11 $ 42.50
		$19.85 $112.34
		$28.72 $ 6.52
		$10.15 $ 14.61

648. Here's a tip. Whenever you have to remember a number with a zero in front, simply use the 's' sound for zero and form a word. 01 — seat; 02 — sun; 03 — seam; 027 — sink; 05 — ___.		soil, sail, seal, soul, etc.
649. For example, to r_____ r $95.04, you could use bell-sore or blazer.		remember
650. Now, do you understand how to r_____ r prices?		remember
651. Simply make words out of the price as per the ph_____ alphabet.		phonetic
652. A_____te the item to the word, or words. Always be sure to actually ___ the picture in your mind.		Associate see

653. You can r_____ r style numbers in exactly the same way.		remember
654. If the style number of a watch is #205, you could a_____te watch to nose-law or to nozzle.		associate
HOW TO REMEMBER TELEPHONE NUMBERS 655. Telephone numbers are no problem either. You can r_____r them just as you do any other numbers.		remember
656. Since all telephone numbers will eventually consist of only numbers (no exchange name), I'll teach you how to r_____r that kind now.		remember
657. When you reach the section of this course that teaches you to remember names and faces, you'll know how to a_____te a telephone number to a name.		associate
658. That will be taught to you in the section on Substitute Words — a method of remembering or ass___-ting names.		associating
659. For now, I'll show you how to remember the telephone numbers of people who can be pictured. You know by now that it's difficult to r_____ r anything that can't be pictured or visualized.		remember
660. Say the carpenter's number is 141-6410. You could a_____e carpenter (man in overalls, holding tools) being very tired (141), lying down and covering himself with shirts (6410).		associate
661. If you actually saw that picture in your mind's eye, you'd always remember the carpenter's telephone number. It is 1__ - ___.		141-6410

662. Had you made a picture of the carpenter trotting (trot — 141) and tearing his clothes to shreds (6410) with his tools, you'd still remember his t_____ number.		telephone
663. You can also use your original Peg Words if you like, and Link them. For example, link carpenter to tire (14); tire to dish (16); dish to rats (410). If you dial 14-16-410, you'll reach the c_____ r.		carpenter
664. I personally find it simpler to make up words covering as many digits as possible. This gives you less words to r_____ r.		remember
665. It is even possible to fit one word to the entire number, occasionally. I.E. — 720-5127; the word, 'consulting' would encompass that entire phone number in our ph____language.		phonetic
666. So, if your dentist's phone number is 720-5127, you could picture him (drill in hand) consulting with everyone. You'd always remember his phone n____ .		number
667. In most instances, however, unless you have plenty of time to think up the long words, it's best to use the shorter words as they come to mind. But do try to get as many numbers into one w___ as possible.		word
668. I've decided that I might take a moment to tell you how to r_____ r the exchange name and number also, since many of you do still have to dial the first two letters of an exchange name.		remember
669. The first word of your a_____tion should remind you of the first two letters of the exchange name and the exchange number.		association
670. The way to do it is this:- The word you select must begin with the first two letters of the exchange name (the two you have to dial). The next consonant s___d must be the one which represents the exchange number in our ph____ alphabet.		sound phonetic

671. Any following consonant s___ds in that word that you make up are ignored or disregarded.		sounds
672. For example: For COlumbus 5, your word must begin with, co. The next consonant s____ must be L, to represent 5. So, coal, cold, colt, collar, colony, etc. would serve the purpose.		sound
673. To repeat, only the CO and the L sound count, in this example. The other consonant s___ s in cold, collar, etc., are ignored here.		sounds
674. For REgent 2, you could use rein, rent, render, etc. Remember that you're only interested in the first two letters and the very next consonant s___ . The sounds after that are disregarded.		sound
675. Of course, the idea is to select a word which can be pictured and which fits the rest of the ass_____n.		association
676. For example, for FLeming 9-2814, see a picture of whoever this number belongs to, flipping a knife into a tire! Flip (FL 9); knife (28) and tire (__).		14
677. The word, 'escape' could represent _____ a) EXeter 4 b) LOngacre 5 c) ESplanade 7 d) ESplanade 1		c) ESplanade 7
678. The word, 'goal' can only represent a) HAnover 5 b) GOrdon 5 c) GAbney 3 d) HIckory 6		b) GOrdon 5
679. CIrcle 7 can be represented by the word a) sickly b) sect c) cigarette d) crack		c) cigarette

76

680. Do you see how this one word can help you to remember the first two letters and the exchange number of any telephone n___r?		number
681. It is only necessary to remember the <u>first t___</u> letters of the exchange name, because those are the only two you have to dial.		two
682. The rest of the number, of course, is remembered as I've already taught you. If the lamp maker's telephone number is DE 4-4203, you could pi___e a <u>deer</u> wearing a lamp on his head, caught in a heavy <u>rain</u> which causes a <u>seam</u> to open on his body.		picture
683. Do you understand why? The lamp in the picture is to represent the lamp maker; <u>deer</u> represents DE 4; <u>rain</u> — 42 and <u>seam</u> — 03. The sillier the p___e or association, the better.		picture
684. The same number, of course, could be remembered by picturing or a___ing the same deer with a lamp instead of antlers being held for <u>ransom</u>.		associating
685. Which telephone number would the following association represent? A gigantic <u>deck</u> of cards is being <u>shuffled</u>. (see next frame)	No answer required.	
685. (continued) a) DE 7-6851 b) DE 6-8615 c) CI 7-5168 d) DO 7-1658		a) DE 7-6851
686. Which telephone number does this picture represent? A gigantic lump of <u>coal</u> is acting like a <u>train</u> and driving through a <u>zoo</u>. (see next frame)	No answer required.	
686. (continued) a) CI 5-1042 b) CO 5-1420 c) DI 4-4201 d) DE 1-2410		b) CO 5-1420

687. Why not take a moment here and see if you can r_____ r all these telephone numbers and who they belong to: (see next frame)		remember
687. (continued) carpenter – 141–6410 doctor – 794–5140 shoemaker – 501–9390 banker – 154–7632 dentist – 720–5127 tailor – 215–0947 baker – 450–1394 TV repairman – 747–1967	**No answer required.**	
688. Now try these: Lamp maker – DE 4–4203 coin store – HI 5–3841 Post office – LI 7–0139 library – RE 1–4263	No answer required.	
689. Have you tried to remember them? If you have, you must agree that your m____y for telephone numbers has improved by 100%!		memory
690. Ordinarily, without the use of my systems, all these numbers would become completely confused in your mind. There's nothing to 'peg' the numbers to. With my P__ method, it becomes a snap.		Peg
691. Again, let me remind you that in actual practice, once you've associated a price, style number or telephone number which you intend to use often enough, the association will soon no longer be important. You've r_____ed the information.		remembered
692. My systems help you to grasp new information originally. They help register the information into your m____y. They are means to an end. When the end is accomplished, the means are unimportant.		memory
693. Now, for a quick review: To remember the price of any item, a_____te the item itself to the (phonetic language) words that fit that price.		associate
694. To remember the style number of any item, associate the item to the w__ds that fit that style number.		words

695. To remember phone numbers, associate the person (or image of the person) to the words that fit that phone n____ .		number
696. Let me pause here for a moment to tell you that whenever I suggest you try something in this course, you should try it. Just reading it will not help your m___y.		memory
697. Just answering all the questions isn't enough either. Try all the things I tell you to. Do this for three reasons; one, for the practice; two, for the incentive. . . you will see that my systems do work; and three, to give you confidence and prove that your m___y is definitely improving.		memory
HOW TO AMAZE YOUR FRIENDS — TONIGHT! 698. Now we come to the most interesting and useful application of the P__ method of memory; remembering long-digit numbers.		Peg
699. Before getting this far in this course, do you think you could have remembered a n____r like this, 522641639527, in a minute or two? I don't think so!		number
700. And, even if you could remember it normally, do you think you'd know it forwards and backwards and r_____r it for as long as you liked? I don't think so!		remember
701. Well, instead of trying to remember twelve unassociated digits, I'll teach you to lock this number in your mind by remembering only six objects or words.	No answer required.	
702. And by now, you know how easy it is to remember a few objects, using my L____ system of memory.		Link
703. Look at, and study, this: 52 26 41 63 95 27 lion notch rod jam bell neck (see next frame)	No answer required.	

703. (continued) Do you see how each word must represent the n___r above it?		number
704. The words could be P___Words you've previously determined, or words you made up as they were needed. In either case, the s___ds in each word must represent the two-digit number above it.		Peg sounds
705. Now, make a L___between lion and notch; notch and rod; rod and jam; jam and bell and bell and neck. Be sure to make the ass_____ns ridiculous, and s___ each picture in your mind. Try it!		Link associations see
706. You could use the following pictures:- see a lion with a large notch in him; see yourself whittling notches into a gigantic curtain r__.		rod
707. See yourself spreading jam on a curtain rod; now you're spreading some jam on a bell, and there's a gigantic and heavy bell around your n___.		neck
708. Once you've made the L___ of these words, you've memorized a twelve-digit number!		Link
709. Simply go over the Link in your mind and say the number indicated by each consonant s___d.		sound
710. Do you see? You've just memorized a complete-ly abstract and intangible long-digit number by making a L___of only six tangible items!		Link
711. And, it isn't necessary to L__ even that many items!		Link

712. You remember that I told you that you can make up w__ds to fit as many digits as you like.		words
713. You could remember 522641639527 this way too:- 522 641 639 527 linen chart jump link (see next frame)	No answer required.	
713. (continued) Do you see? Each word now represents three digits. So you can remember this twelve-digit number by Linking only four w__ds!		words
714. The thing to do is to look at any long-digit number and make up the words for as many digits at a time as you can. Just make sure that the s__ds fit the n__rs.		sounds numbers
715. Sometimes you may be stuck at one digit. Then simply use your original P__ Word for that single digit.		Peg
716. On the other hand, if you have the time to find w__s that take in more digits, that's fine.		words
717. The important thing is that instead of trying to remember meaningless numbers, you're remembering m_____ful pictures.		meaningful
718. If you had the time to think of 'jumbling,' you could have remembered 522641639527 by making a L__ of only three words! 522 641 639527 linen chart jumbling		Link
719. How would you r_____r this number, 994614757954? It's simple. 994 614 757 954 paper ashtray clock bowler (see next frame)		remember

719. (continued) piper jitter click blower pauper shudder cloak player	No answer required.	
720. Here's a formidable looking number, 42109483521461279071. Very few people would even attempt to r_____r that.		remember
721. But look at it now: <u>7210</u> <u>9483</u> <u>5214</u> <u>6127</u> <u>9071</u> rents perfume launder shouting basket (see next frame)	No answer required.	
721. (continued) All you have to do is L___ five words and you've remembered a twenty-digit number!		Link
722. You needn't break the numbers into even groups. I'm just doing that for explanation purposes. Just start at the beginning of the n____r and make up words and L___them as they come to you.		number Link
723. For example:- <u>0195</u> <u>910</u> <u>2</u> <u>749527</u> staple beds Noah crippling You see, the n_____s do not have to be in even groups at all.		numbers
724. You can use this method to show off to your friends right now! Have them write a long-digit number on a piece of paper, and then simply L ___it forwards and backwards!		Link
725. You know you can remember a L___of items backwards, so there's no reason why you can't remember a long-digit number backwards.		Link
726. Simply start with your last item and go backwards to the first, translating sounds into n____rs as you go! You can't help but remember the numbers backwards!		numbers

82

727. Incidentally, if you made a L___ of the first list of items I taught you at the beginning of this programed course, carpet to car, you memorized this number!! 7491994915918664218540741251941469212174		Link
728. Unbelievable!? I think so. Do you see the importance of knowing the s___ds of the ph____ alphabet now?		sounds phonetic
729. To remember any long-digit number, simply break the number into words and L___the words.		Link
730. Be sure that each word contains only the s___ds that represent the numbers you're interested in.		sounds
731. Now you can remember long-digit numbers as you never have before because of my P__ and L____ systems of memory.		Peg Link
732. Before I teach you how to remember names and faces, why not see if you can r_____r these long-digit n___rs. 7415270139 28497011502041 37029410785 95247380126		remember numbers
733. Well, if you've come this far with me, and if you've answered all the questions, I know you now agree that you have vastly improved your m_____.		memory
734. You can already r_____ r as you've never done before.		remember
735. I would strongly suggest that you thoroughly understand the L___and P___systems before going on to names and faces.		Link Peg

HOW TO REMEMBER NAMES AND FACES.

736. Although the system for remembering names and faces has little to do with the Peg and Link, it does have to do with ridiculous a_____ns.		associations
737. I don't think I have to tell you that the biggest memory problem of our time is remembering names and ____s.		faces
738. Most of us recognize the face; it's the n___ that gives us trouble.		name
739. That's because most of us are 'eye-minded.' We remember what we s___ better than what we hear.		see
740. Since most of us recognize, or remember, faces, why not take advantage of that fact and, in some way, tie the name to the f___?		face
741. Many of you may have seen me perform personally, or on the Jack Paar, Johnny Carson or Ed Sullivan shows. If you have, you've seen me r_____ r up to seven hundred names and f___s at one time!		remember faces
742. I can do this (and I do it almost every day at private performances) because of a simple system that does the work for me, and will work for you as well. You too, can remember n___s and f___s.		names faces
743. Of course, I realize that you do not necessarily want to r_____ r up to seven hundred names and faces every day. You do, however, want to remember the people you meet daily in business and socially.		remember
744. All right. Before going into the actual system, let me better your m_____y for names and faces by 25% by giving you some simple rules.		memory

745. Most people forget names because they never <u>remembered</u> them in the first place! You don't <u>forget</u> the n___ , you just never took the time and effort to commit it to m_____y.		name memory
746. As a matter of fact, half the time you don't even <u>hear</u> the name properly, so how <u>can</u> you re_____ it?		remember
747. People love to hear their own names, so don't be embarrassed to ask them to repeat it. You'll flatter them if you do. Be absolutely sure you hear the n ___!		name
748. The first rule then, is: Be sure to h ___ the name when you're being introduced.		hear
749. If you're not sure of the spelling, try to s___l it and you'll be corrected. This will help to fix it into your memory.		spell
750. I repeat, it is flattering to make a fuss over another person's name. Do not be embarrassed to ask to h__r it again or to try to sp___ it.		hear spell
751. The second rule then, is: If you're not sure of the spelling; spell it, or have the person s___ it for you.		spell
752. If there is any odd fact about the name, or if it is similar to a n___ you know, mention it. The person will be pleased to discuss it.		name
753. During the course of your initial conversation, be it short or long, <u>repeat</u> the name as often as you can. Remember to r____t the name.		repeat

754. Finally, always use the name when you say good-bye. Don't just say, good-bye; say good-bye, Mr. so and so! Remember to always use the_____when you say good-bye.		name
755. Basically, all these rules are accomplishing one main thing. They are forcing you to be _interested_ in the person's name. And, as I said before, i_____t is an essential part of memory.		interest
756. So remember to apply the rules. Be sure to h___ the person's name.		hear
757. If you're not sure of the spelling, try to s___ the name.		spell
758. If there's any odd fact about the n___, or if it's familiar to you, mention it.		name
759. Always r___t the name as often as possible during the conversation.		repeat
760. Be sure to use the n___when you say good-bye.		name
761. If you apply these few rules religiously, you will immediately better your m____y for n_____ and faces by at least 25%.		memory names
762. Now let's take care of the remaining 75%. If you apply the system I'm about to teach you, you should never again forget a n___ or a f___.		name face

763. To simplify the process, you will learn first, what to do with the name, and then, how to associate the n___ to the f___ .		name face
764. Actually they go hand in hand. If the system you're about to learn is applied correctly, the name will conjure up the face for you, and the f___ will bring the n___ to mind.		face name
HOW TO TURN NAMES INTO PICTURES 765. All right; first the names. As mentioned before, the most difficult things to r_____r are abstracts and intangibles.		remember
766. There is nothing more abstract and/or intangible than most names. Usually, n___s have no meaning at all to you.		names
767. Of course, there are many n___s that do have meaning, such as, Carpenter, Green, Cook, Fox, Coyne, Brown, etc.		names
768. Names like these, that already have m_____g present no problem.		meaning
769. Then there are other n___s that may not have a definite meaning, but will suggest or create a picture in your mind.		names
770. For example, there are names like, Jordan (the River Jordan); Sullivan (John L. Sullivan, prize fighter); Lincoln (President of the U.S.A.), etc. This category of n___s creates no problem either.		names
771. The n___s that <u>do</u> create a problem are those that have no meaning at all and create no picture in your mind.		names

772. So, I will teach you my system which I call, <u>Substitute Words</u>. This is simply a method of making meaningless and intangible names m_____ful and t____le.		meaningful tangible
773. The Substitute Word system is this:- Upon coming across a n___ which is intangible and meaningless to you, you simply find a word, phrase or thought that sounds as close to the name as possible, and that <u>is</u> tangible and m_____ful.		name meaningful
774. <u>Any</u> word that you ever have to remember that is meaningless, can be made easier to remember if you create a S_____e Word for it that is meaningful and intelligible.		Substitute
775. Any name, no matter how long or odd-sounding and meaningless can be made to create a meaningful picture in your mind if you use my system of Substitute W___s.		Words
776. For example: The name, Freedman, although not uncommon or difficult, really means nothing until you think of a man being fried (fried man — Freedman), or a man waving an American flag — he's free, (free man — Freedman). These things can be pic___ed in your mind.		pictured
777. For the name, Fishter, you could picture a fish stirring something (fish stir — Fishter), or, see yourself tearing a fish in half (fish tear — Fishter). These things, or actions, can be p_____ed, whereas the name itself cannot.		pictured
778. Some of you may want to simply picture a fish for Fishter. That would do it for some of you. As I told you before, r_____r the main thought and the incidentals will fall into place by true memory!		remember
779. You realize, of course, that in applying the system of Substitute Words you are actually <u>forcing</u> yourself, without pain, to get to h__r the name right in the first place!		hear
780. You <u>cannot</u> apply the Substitute W___ system if you do not hear the n___ correctly.		Word name

781. The very fact that you are thinking of the name, in order to create the S_____ e Word, will help impress the n___ on your mind.		Substitute name
782. You have automatically become interested in the name merely by searching for a S_____ W___ for it.		Substitute Word
783. I recently met a man whose name was Olczewsky, pronounced ol-chew-ski. I simply pictured an old man chewing vigorously on a ski. Old-chew-ski — Olczewsky. See how the name has become m_____ ful?		meaningful
784. For the name, Ettinger, you could picture someone having eaten or 'et' and injured himself. Et injure — Ettinger. Silly? Yes, of course. But it does make the name m_____l.		meaningful
785. Please keep in mind that the pictures you use are a matter of individual choice. The Substitute W___ that comes to you first is the one to use.		Word
786. I'll give you examples of the S_____ Words that I may use, but that doesn't mean that you have to use them too. You use whatever brings the name to mind for you.		Substitute
787. Some more ideas and examples: For the name, Smith, I always picture a blacksmith swinging his hammer. For Cohen, Cohn or Cohan, I p___re an ice cream cone. For Gordon or Gardner, picture a garden.		picture
788. For Berg — ice berg. For any name ending in 'witz', (Liebowitz, Shomowitz) picture brains for wits. For names ending in 'ly,' (O'Mally, etc.) p___re a meadow, or lea. For words ending in 'ler,' (Chandler, (see next frame)		picture
788. (continued) Handler) you might picture either a policeman or a judge's gavel to represent law.	No answer required.	

789. If you have a very close friend named, Williams, you can picture him when you meet someone else named Williams. Or, picture sweet potatoes (yams) writing their wills. Will yams — W_____ .		Williams
790. These are all examples of S_____W___s or thoughts.		Substitute Words
791. The following frames will be used to give you more examples of Substitute W__ds or thoughts for some names which ordinarily would be completely abstract and meaningless. Please study them carefully and see if they are the words you would select.		Words
792. Steinwurtzel: Picture a beer stein worth selling. Stein worth sell = _____ .		Steinwurtzel
793. McCarthy: I always picture the famous ventrilo-quial dummy, Charlie McCarthy, for this name. Or, picture a Mack truck carting tea. Ventriloquial dummy or Mack cart tea = _____.		McCarthy
794. Brady: Picture a girl's braids; or, you're braid-ing the lines of a large letter E. Braid E =_____ .		Brady
795. Moreida: You could picture yourself reading and calling for more and more books to read. Or, your maw (mother) is a big reader. Maw reader, more reader = _____ .		Moreida
796. Carruthers: Picture a car with cow's udders. Car udders = _____ .		Carruthers
797. Kolodny: You might see a large knee that's all different colors. Colored knee =_____ .		Kolodny

798. Kolcyski: Either a piece of coal skiing in a sitting position, or, it's too cold to stand and ski, so you sit and ski. Coal sit ski, cold sit ski = _____ .		Kolcyski
799. Zauber: See yourself sawing a bear in half, or sawing in the nude. Saw bear, saw bare = _____ .		Zauber
800. Zimmerman: Picture a man cooking or simmering in a large pot. (I mean the man is _in_ the pot.) Simmer man = _____ .		Zimmerman
801. Platinger: Picturing a plate with an injury (all bandaged up) would do it. Plate injure = _____ .		Platinger
802. Casselwitz: You might see a castle so full of brains (wits) that they're oozing out of all the windows. Castle wits = _____ .		Casselwitz
803. Pukczyva, pronounced, puk-shiv-a: This difficult name is made easy to remember by picturing a hockey puck so cold that it's shivering. Puck shiver = _____ .		Pukczyva
804. Smolensky: A small camera (lens) is skiing. Small lens ski = _____ .		Smolensky
805. There you are. It's easy, isn't it? There are sometimes many different S_____ Words or thoughts which would suffice for any particular name.		Substitute
806. The one you think of first is usually best. If the S_____ W____ brings the name to mind for you, then it's a good one.		Substitute Word

807. Only some practice and experience will prove to you that there is no name, no matter how strange sounding or lengthy, which cannot be broken down into a S_____W____or thought.		Substitute Word
808. Always keep in mind that your Substitute W_ds do not have to be exact. If it brings the main element of the name to mind, that will suffice.		Words
809. For example: A pic__e of a bell would probably be enough to remind you of the name Belden. Although you could see a bell in a lion's den if you liked. And 'whole nickel' could remind you of Hulnick, although 'hull nick' is closer.		picture
810. Before looking at the next frame, see if you can think of S_____ W___s or thoughts for these names:- Briskin, Hayduk, Citron, Welling, Robinson, Kusik, Stapleton, Fawcett, Krakauer.		Substitute Words
811. Did you think of a S_____W___ for each of those names? If you had any trouble, look at these:- brisk skin — Briskin; hay duck — Hayduk; sit run —· Citron; well ink — Welling; robin son — Robinson; cue sick — Kusik; staple ton — Stapleton; faucet — Fawcett; crack hour (clock) — Krakauer.		Substitute Word
812. All right, if you understand the principle of S_____W___s, let's get to the more important part of the system. How to associate names to faces.		Substitute Words
813. Before we do, however, I just want to remind you that now you can a _____te people's names to telephone numbers.		associate
814. If you want to r_____r that Mr. Rosenbaum's telephone number is HI 6-6072, you might see a gigantic rose dressed as a bum (rose bum — Rosenbaum) who keeps hitching (HI 6) up his pants to show his shoes (60) which are really large coins (72).		remember
815. Mr. Stein's phone number is LE 7-9472. S__ a leg (LE 7) coming out of a gigantic beer stein. The leg is obviously and horribly broken (9472).		See

816. Or, you see the leg coming out of the stein and you break (947) the knee (2). Do you see how to a_____te the name to the number?		associate
817. If my (Mr. Lorayne) phone number were DO 5-3340, you could pic__re dolls (DO 5) that look like judges raining (judge or law, rain — Lorayne) all over you. The dolls have fantastic memories (3340)!		picture
818. Or, p___re the little judge dolls as wrapped like mummies (33) and holding roses (40).		picture
819. Any time you want to remember a name in conjunction with anything else, use the S_____ W____ system.		Substitute Word
820. Even if someone owes you money! Mr. Campbell owes you $12.00. P___re a large piece of tin (12) eating from a can of Campbell soup. Or, a camel (Campbell) is made of tin.		picture
821. Now then, back to names and faces. You realize that if it were possible to force you to really pay attention to n___s always, and to really look at and pay attention to f___s, there just would be no memory problem with names and faces.		names faces
822. Utilizing my idea of S_____ W___s takes care of the names. Now we must do the same for the faces.		Substitute Words
823. The only way to remember n___s and f___s is to associate the person's name to his face in some ridiculous way.		names faces
824. The S_____W___ idea has given you something to associate to the person's face.		Substitute Word

825. Now, how do you a_____e the Substitute Word to the face? Simple. Whenever you meet someone new, look at his face and try to find one outstanding feature!		associate
826. This one o_____ing feature can be anything; small eyes; large eyes; thick or thin lips; low or high forehead; lines or creases on forehead or face; long or broad nose; narrow or wide nostrils; clefts, dimples, (see next frame)		outstanding
826. (continued) warts; small, large or outstanding ears; large or small chin — anything!	No answer required.	
827. You are to select the one thing that is o_____ing to you. Someone else may select something entirely different.		outstanding
828. What you select may not be the o_____ing feature, but the thing that stands out to you at first is the thing that will be obvious and outstanding when you see that face again.		outstanding
829. The essential point here is that aside from finding the outstanding feature, you're of necessity, paying attention to, and being interested in the person's f___.		face
830. The person's face is being etched into your memory simply by trying to work the system, and finding that o_____ing feature.		outstanding
831. When you've decided on the outstanding feature, you're ready to associate the name to that particular part of the f___.		face
832. Say you meet a Mr. Sachs. Mr. Sachs has a very high forehead. You might see millions of sacks falling out of his forehead. Or; see his forehead as a sack instead of a f_____d.		forehead

833. Remember that the picture must be ridiculous and/or illogical and you must actually ___ it in your mind's eye.		see
834. You realize that you're to use the same laws and principles as you've already been taught in this course. They worked for you before, and they'll work for you in solving the problem of remembering names and ___s.		faces
835. Making up S_____ W___s for the names and finding an outstanding feature on the face are easy. The most essential thing is to actually <u>see</u> the picture in your mind's eye.		Substitute Words
836. Look at Mr. Sach's face and you must actually ___ the picture of millions of <u>sacks</u> falling out of his forehead. That's all there is to it!		see
837. If you meet a Mr. Robrum who has a large nose as his o_____ing feature, you might picture his nose as a bottle of rum and a robber stealing it. Rob rum — Robrum.		outstanding
838. Mr. Galloway has a cleft in his chin. See the p____e of a girl (gal) going or falling away, out of that cleft. Gal away — Galloway.		picture
839. Miss Van Nuys has bulging eyes. See two large vans making lots of noise, coming out of those bulging eyes. Van noise — _____		Van Nuys
840. You meet a Mr. Cohen. Mr. Cohen has extremely heavy eyebrows. Look at his face and actually ____ a picture of ice cream cones <u>instead</u> of his eyebrows. See the ice cream dripping into his eyes!		see
841. There is really only one way to practice this and prove to yourself that it works. That is to go ahead and <u>do</u> it. Just reading this won't help; you have to actually go ahead and __ it!		do

842. Although newspaper and magazine pictures are one-dimensional, you can use them for practice. Cut out many pictures of faces and use them as practice cards. Give the pictures names, or use their own, and apply my s____ms.		systems
843. You'll find your m____y for names and faces improved by a great percentage already! Why not try it right now? In each of the next fifteen double frames I'll give you a picture of a face; I'll help you make up S_____ W___s and find the o_____ing features.		memory Substitute Words outstanding
844. All you'll have to do is make the ass_____n for each one and actually ___ it in your mind's eye. Unfortunately, I can't do that for you!		association see
845. Here we go: This is Mr. Carpenter. The name is no problem because it already has meaning. If you look closely, you'll see a scar (see next frame)		
845. on Mr. Carpenter's right cheek; also he has a very small mouth. Pick the one which is most outstanding to you and a _____te carpenter to that. (see next frame)		associate
846. You might see a carpenter working on the small mouth (get the tools; hammer, saw, etc. into the picture) trying to make it larger. (see next frame)		
846. Or; the carpenter is trying to repair the scar. Whichever you choose, look at the face and actually ___ the picture in your mind's eye.		see
847. This is Mr. Brimler. See the deep dimples in his cheeks? You can see those dimples being brim (see next frame)		
847. full of judges' gavels (law). Be sure to see the picture. Brim law= _____.		Brimler

	848. This is Miss Standish. Her 'bang' hairdo is the first thing that strikes me about her face. See many people <u>standing</u> in the hairdo and (see next frame)		
	848. scratching violently because they <u>itch</u>. Look at Miss Standish and <u>see</u> the picture. Stand itch = _____.		Standish
	849. This is Mr. Smolensky. He has a very broad nose (or a double chin). See someone <u>skiing</u> on the nose and taking pictures of it with (see next frame)		
	849. a <u>small</u> camera (<u>lens</u>). Be sure to actually see the action in the picture. Small lens ski =_____.		Smolensky
	850. This is Mr. Hecht. See the ridiculous picture of his mustache being violently <u>hacked</u> from his face. Violence and action make the pic- (see next frame)		
	850. tures easier to recall. Be sure to look at the face and see the picture. Hacked =_____.		Hecht
	851. This is Mrs. Bjornsen, pronounced Byorn – son. Look at Mrs. Bjornsen and try to actually visualize a boy (son) being born in the very (see next frame)		
	851. wide part in her hair! Born son =_____.		Bjornsen
	852. We've already met Miss Van Nuys. Look at her bulging eyes. See some moving vans driving out of those eyes, making terribly loud (see next frame)		

852. noises. So loud, you have to hold your ears. See the picture. Van noise = _____.		Van Nuys
853. This is Mr. Hamper. You can use his very wide mouth as the outstanding feature. See yourself cramming all your dirty clothes into his (see next frame)		
853. mouth because it's a hamper. Look at Mr. Hamper and actually ____ this picture in your mind.		see
854. This is Miss Smith. A common name, but just as easy to forget as an uncommon one if no association is made. Miss Smith's lips are very (see next frame)		
854. full. They appear to be swollen. See a blacksmith swinging his hammer at those lips, causing them to swell. Be sure to ____ the picture.		see
855. Here's Mr. Kannen. You might select his outstanding ear, or the lines in the corner of his eye, or the thin long mouth as the outstanding feature. Whichever you select, (see next frame)		
855. you can picture a cannon either shooting from the feature, or shooting it off. Be sure to actually see the picture. Cannon = _____.		Kannen
856. This is Mr. D'Amico. You can't miss the full head of wavy hair. See this hair as a gigantic dam. The water is overflowing as you scream 'eek' and 'oh.' (see next frame)		
856. Or; you're running toward the dam, shouting 'me go.' See the picture. Dam eek oh, dam me go = _____.		D'Amico

857. This is Miss Forrester. I would picture trees (forest) growing out of those heavy, definite lines on her lower cheeks. If you want to (see next frame)		
857. get the last syllable into the association, see the forest tearing her cheeks. Forest tear = _____.		Forrester
858. Here is Mr. Pfeffer. The P is silent. Look at his cleft chin. See lots and lots of pepper coming out of (see next frame)		
858. it, making him (and you) sneeze. Look at Mr. Pfeffer and ___ the picture.		see
859. Remember, it's not enough to just read and answer my questions in these frames. You must actually ___ the association in your mind's eye if you want to remember these names and faces.		see
860. This is Mr. Silverberg. He has a strong, jutting chin. Look at the face and see a large silver iceberg instead of his jutting chin. (see next frame)		
860. Actually see it glittering and you'll get the idea of silver in there. Silver berg = _____.		Silverberg
861. Finally, here is Miss Kornfeld. Look at that very wide mouth. I would see millions (exaggeration) of ears of corn falling from her (see next frame)		
862. mouth. Be sure to actually see the picture in your mind. Corn fell = _____.		Kornfeld

863. I've purposely used a wide assortment of names to show that it makes no difference. If you made the ass_____ns strong and ridiculous enough, and most important, if you actually saw the pictures, you should remember most of these people.		associations
864. I've also purposely used the same o_____ing feature twice, to show that that makes no difference either.		outstanding
865. Remember, it's the fact that you're <u>looking</u> for that o_____ing feature, and tying the name, or Substitute Word for the name, to it, that's important.		outstanding
866. Naturally, in meeting many people, you will be using the same outstanding feature again and again. It makes no difference because in looking for that f____re, you're etching the face into your mind.		feature
867. In the next fifteen frames, I'll repeat the pictures of these same people in a different order. Write the correct n___ in each blank. You will see if you're correct as you move to each successive frame.		name
868. Look at each face. The same feature you thought was outstanding before should strike you immediately now. Look at this o_____ing feature and the association you made will come back to you, supplying the name like a filing cabinet.		outstanding
869. This is Mr. _____.		Hamper
870. This is Miss _____.		Forrester
871. This is Miss _____.		Kornfeld

100

872.		This is Miss ____.		Smith
873.		This is Mr. _____.		D'Amico
874.		This is Mr. _____.		Pfeffer
875.		This is Miss _____.		Standish
876.		This is Mr. _____.		Silverberg
877.		This is Mr. _____.		Kannen
878.		This is Mrs. _____.		Bjornsen
879.		This is Mr. _____.		Smolensky
880.		This is Mr. _____.		Brimler

881. This is Mr. ____.			Hecht
882. This is Mr. _____.			Carpenter
883. This is Miss _____.			Van Nuys
884. Did you get most of the names right? Did you miss a few ____s? If you did, that's all right – I expected you to! I expected you to forget a few names for a variety of reasons.			names
885. First of all, it is more difficult to visualize one-dimensional pictures than a real person. Second, it would be better if you looked at the faces and searched for the o_____ing feature yourself.			outstanding
886. The fact that I pointed out the outstanding features for you, did not help you get a subconscious picture of the entire f___ in your mind. ·			face
887. Well now, you've met quite a few people all at once for the first time you're trying this technique. Also, had you actually met these people, you'd have had time to see the people on and off and check your ass_____ns, and 'rap' in the names.			associations
888. So you see, I didn't expect you to r_____r them all. If you did, or if you missed only one or two, you're doing excellently.			remember
889. If you go back and strengthen your ass_____ns on those you missed, you'll have them all now.			associations

890. I can only repeat, the best way to practice this system is to <u>do</u> it and use it. Next time you meet someone new, <u>try</u> my systems, you'll amaze yourself. Your m____y for names and faces will surprise even you.		memory
891. If you meet a large group of people, such as at a cocktail party, apply my systems with each person you're introduced to. Then as you see the people again during the evening, the n___s should come right into your mind.		names
892. This serves to 'rap' the names into your m____y. When meeting new people during the regular business day, apply the systems. Later on, when you have the time, think of their faces and the names will come to mind. This serves as review.		memory
893. You'll find that after the names are etched into your m____y, your original association may fade, but you'll always know the name.		memory
894. The important thing is to get over the hump of actually putting my m____y systems to work. Put them to work; use them and they will diligently work for you!		memory
895. At first, you may feel that my system for remembering names and ____s takes too much time.		faces
896. Try it, and you'll see that it does not. After a bit of practice, you'll be able to think of a Substitute Word for the ___, and find an o_____ing feature on the face, and associate them in less time than it usually takes to say, 'hello.'		name outstanding
897. Before going into the final review, I want to mention one or two other facts. Keep in mind that I've given you only the 'meat' of my m____y systems.		memory
898. They can be manipulated and twisted and molded to solve <u>any</u> m____y problem that can ever come up.		memory

899. This may take a bit of imagination on your part. Of course, without your realizing it, applying my systems has improved not only your m____y, but also your sense of observation, concentration and <u>imagination</u>.		memory
900. Making up Substitute W___s for names and looking for o_____ing features on faces has 'forced' you to observe, concentrate and use your imagination.		Words outstanding
901. Making up r_____s associations for the Peg and Link methods and for names and faces has certainly made you exercise your imagination and 'creative thinking' abilities.		ridiculous
902. To think creatively means to think along <u>new</u> paths; paths you've never explored before. This, of course, takes imagination. My m____y systems have started you exploring along paths you've never dreamed existed.		memory
903. If you haven't realized it yet, <u>all</u> m____y is really based on <u>one</u> important point. And that is, that anything to be remembered must <u>register</u> in your mind.		memory
904. This goes hand in hand with observation. If you do not observe something, whether heard, seen or felt, and if it doesn't r____ter in your mind, how can it <u>possibly</u> be remembered?		register
905. Any new piece of information, if <u>originally</u> grasped and registered is already half r_____red.		remembered
906. Go over my systems and you'll see that they're based on one thing. They force you (painlessly, since we're all basically lazy), to observe and <u>register</u> anything you wish to r_____r.		remember
907. Now, before going too much farther into the subject of mind organization, or mind power, let's review all we know about my m____y systems.		memory

908. All memory is based on a_____n.		association
909. It is easier to remember violent, silly, illogical or r_____s associations than it is to remember pleasant or logical ones.		ridiculous
910. The system which enables you to remember things in sequence only is called the a) Link method b) Peg method		a) Link method
911. The system which enables you to rememeber things in and out of order <u>and</u> in sequence is called the a) Link method b) Peg method		b) Peg method
912. The most important thing about any association is to a) write it down b) love it c) see it in your mind (see next frame)		
912. (continued) d) forget it		c) see it in your mind
913. The Link method teaches us to always associate the new piece of information to the last piece of in_____, or the present to the <u>previous</u>.		information
914. Associating the present item to the previous item as in the Link method forms a sturdy mental ch_ _n of all the items.		chain
915. In the Link method, once we've associated two items, we stop thinking about that association and proceed to the n_ _t one.		next

916. The basis of the Peg method is the ph _____ alphabet.		phonetic
917. The sounds of the phonetic alphabet aid us in forming P___ W___ s.		Peg Words
918. The sounds of the phonetic alphabet also are of great value in remembering n____rs of any kind.		numbers
919. To remember style numbers, telephone numbers, long-digit numbers, we use the P___ method of memory.		Peg
920. To remember a telephone number we must associate the person to the number with the help of P___ W___ s or the sounds of the phonetic alphabet.		Peg Words
921. To remember a shopping list we use the L ___ method of memory.		Link
922. You can use either, or both, the Peg or Link methods to r_____r your errands and appointments, speeches, jokes, etc.		remember
923. To remember the exchange name and number of a telephone number we must use a word which begins with the first ___ letters of the exchange name.		two
924. The very next consonant sound in this word must be the sound which represents the exchange n____r.		number

925. It is best to remember a speech or article _____ for _____ , not word for word.		thought thought
926. In order to remember a speech with my methods, we must select a K___W___ from each thought of the speech.		Key Word
927. In order to remember a long-digit number forwards and backwards we use a combination of the P___ and Link methods of memory.		Peg
928. The numbers themselves are retained via the P___ method; and their sequence, via the Link method.		Peg
929. A word to represent the #9751 would be a) booklet b) magazine c) brakes d) bagatelle		a) booklet
930. A word for the exchange name and number CI 7, could be a) circle b) curve c) cigarette d) kick		c) cigarette
931. The only way to remember names and faces is to associate the name to the _____.		face
932. If we associate the name to the face properly and in some ridiculous way, the face will bring the _____ to mind when we see it again.		name
933. Any name can be made tangible and meaningful with the use of S_____ W____ s.		Substitute Words

934. A Substitute Word is simply a word, phrase or thought which can be pictured and which s_____s like the name we want to remember.		sounds
935. In order to associate the name to the face, we must look for one o_____ing feature on the person's face.		outstanding
936. The name, or the Substitute Word for the name, is associated to that _____ing feature in a ridiculous way.		outstanding
937. To remember a person's telephone number, we would a_____e the Substitute Word for his name to his telephone number.		associate
938. If you want to remember anything, it must first register in your mind. You cannot remember anything you do not ob_____.		observe
939. My memory systems will strengthen your sense of observation, concentration and im_____.		imagination
940. Aside from actually learning my systems, the most important thing is for you to try them and to u___them.		use
941. If you don't try them, and more important, use them, you'll never really know if they can work for you, will you? So please,___the systems!!		use
942. Incidentally, after using my systems for a while, they'll become almost second nature and you'll use them almost without thinking. Make them a habit! U___the systems!		Use

IMPORTANT NOTE: A SPECIAL BONUS SEC-
TION BEGINS ON THE NEXT SHEET.

No answer required.

BONUS SECTION: HOW TO MASTER FOREIGN LANGUAGES

943. Just one final example of how manipulating my m ___ y systems can be useful for practical purposes.		memory
944. There isn't anything you can't r_____r easier, better and with more retentiveness if you will apply my systems to it.		remember
945. My system of Substitute W___ s can be of great value in remembering foreign language vocabulary.		Words
946. The system for remembering foreign language vocabulary breaks down to simply this:- You must a _____the foreign word to its English meaning.		associate
947. Of course, there is nothing more abstract and/or intangible than a foreign (to you) word. You have already learned, however, how to make any meaningless word (or name) m_____ful.		meaningful
948. Why not use a S _____ W___ in order to make any foreign word tangible and meaningful?		Substitute Word
949. It's easy! First, handle the foreign word exactly as if it were a person's n___. Invent a Substitute Word for it, just as you did with names.		name
950. Then all you have to do is to a _____e the Substitute Word for the foreign word to its English meaning.		associate
951. All right; let's try it. Remember, in order to make a foreign word tangible and meaningful, use my system of S _____ W___ s.		Substitute Words

110

952. The Spanish word for 'bird' is 'pajaro,' pronounced pa-car-o. A S_____ Word for that could be 'parked car.'		Substitute
953. Since 'pajaro' means 'bird' simply a_____ parked car to bird in a ridiculous manner.		associate
954. You might picture a parked car crammed full of birds, or, a gigantic b__ is parking a car, etc.		bird
955. But why don't you make each picture or _____tion as we go on? Later on, I'll test you on all the foreign words I've used as examples.		association
956. In that way, I can prove to you that you can r_____r foreign language vocabulary with the use of my systems.		remember
957. Have you made the ridiculous a_____n between, or with, bird and parked car? Remember, you must actually see the picture.		association
958. Let me remind you that the S_____ W___ I use is not necessarily the best one for you.		Substitute Word
959. Just as I told you when I taught you to make up Substitute Words for names, you are to use whatever comes to your mind first. The only rule is that it must s___d as close to the foreign word as possible.		sound
960. I won't go into too much detail here since I have already done so in teaching you how to make up S_____ W___s for names.		Substitute Words

961. Just remember that if you get the <u>main</u> part of the foreign word into your a_____n, that's all you'll need.		association
962. All right. "Ventana' means 'window' in Spanish. A S_____ W___ or thought for 'ventana' might be a girl (whom you know) whose name is Anna, and 'vent.'		Substitute Word
963. Now this (vent Anna) must be associated to window. Simply p___re Anna violently throwing vents (air vents or ventriloquists) through a closed window. Be sure to see the picture. See the vents going through that w_____.		picture window
964. The <u>French</u> word for window is, 'fenetre.' You could picture a window eating a raw fan; or a fan eating a raw window. Fan ate raw = _____.		fenetre
965. So pick one of those associations, and be sure to actually ___ it in your mind's eye.		see
966. The Spanish word, 'hermano,' pronounced air-mon-o, means 'brother.' Just picture your brother as an airman. Be sure to ___ the picture. See the airman's wings on your b____. They're <u>gigantic</u> wings.		see brother
967. The Spanish word for 'room' is, 'cuarto, pronounced quart-o. Simply make an a_____n between room and, say, quarter.		association
968. A room piled high and completely filled with quarters would do it. Be sure to actually ___ the picture in your mind. See the quarters filling that r___.		see room
969. 'Vasa' means 'glass' in Spanish. See yourself drinking from a gigantic <u>vase</u> instead of a g___.		glass

970. The word for 'bridge' in French is, 'pont.' See yourself punting a football on or over a bridge. Or, you're punting a b____ instead of a football.		bridge
971. 'Pluma' means 'pen' in Spanish. See yourself writing with a gigantic plume instead of a pen; or, you're writing on a gigantic plume with a leaky ___ .		pen
972. The French word for 'father' is, 'pere.' A____te father to pear (the fruit) and you won't forget it.		Associate
973. You might see your father eating a gigantic (bigger than he) pear, or, a gigantic pear is rocking you to sleep; it's your f____ !		father
974. If you've made all the associations as I've suggested, using your own Substitute W___s and pictures, you should have no trouble filling in the following blanks.		Words
975. For example, 'pajaro' sounds like 'parked car.' When you hear the word you'll think of that and you'll remember that you associated a parked car with a ___ .		bird
976. Therefore, you'll always remember that 'pajaro' is the Spanish word for ___ .		bird
977. The Spanish word, 'ventana' means _____ .		window
978. The French word, 'fenetre' also means _____ .		window

979. The Spanish word, 'hermano' means _____.		brother
980. The Spanish word, 'cuarto' means ____.		room
981. The Spanish word, 'vasa' means ____.		glass
982. The French word, 'pont' means ____.		bridge
983. The Spanish word, 'pluma' means ___.		pen
984. The French word, 'pere' means ____.		father
985. Now try this: - The Spanish word for 'pen' is ____.		pluma
986. The Spanish word for 'brother' is _____.		hermano
987. The French word for 'bridge' is ___.		pont

988. Window (French) is _____.		fenetre
Glass (Spanish) is ____.		vasa
Father (French) is _____.		pere
989. Bird (Spanish) is ____.		pajaro
Room (Spanish) is ____.		quarto
Window (Spanish) is _____.		ventano
990. Did you get them all? If your associations were strong enough and r_____s enough, you <u>must</u> have answered them all correctly.		ridiculous
991. Do you realize that you've just thoroughly r_____d nine f_____ words and their English meanings after hearing them or seeing them only once?		remembered foreign
992. I have, of course, used simple words; the first ones that came to me. I suggest you try this system the next time you have to remember <u>any</u> f_____ word or words.		foreign
993. Aside from foreign languages, my system can be used for anything you may be studying which entails r_____ing words which have no meaning to you, at first.		remembering
994. A medical student, for example, can r_____ the word, 'femur' if he associates <u>fee more</u> to whatever it is it must be associated to.		remember
995. The same is true for sacrum (sack of rum); fibula (fib you lie); patella (pat Ella or pay teller); coccyx (cock (rooster) kicks or cock sics). Do you see how the S_____ W___s make these words easier to remember?		Substitute Words
996. A pharmaceutical student might picture or a_____e someone pushing a large <u>bell down</u> over him while he <u>throws pine</u> trees from under it, in order to remember that atropine (I throw pine) comes from the belladonna (bell down) root or leaf.		associate

997. Remember; with a bit of thought you can make up much better Substitute Words. For example, you could picture a giver (donor) of a bell to r_____r, or remind you of, belladonna!		remember
998. If you always keep in mind that it is much easier to remember pictures than intangibles, you'll always use my system of S_____W___s to help you remember foreign words or any words which have no meaning to you at first.		Substitute Words
999. To remember a foreign word and its English meaning, you must a_____e the Substitute Word for the foreign word to its English meaning.		associate
1000. In this way, the foreign word will always bring the English meaning to mind, and more important, the English meaning will bring the f_____ word to mind.		foreign
You have now completed Course #1 of Harry Lorayne's <u>Instant Mind Power</u> Teaching-Machine. Course #2 Begins on the next sheet.	No answer required.	
	↑ ↑	
	↑ ↑	
	↑ ↑	
	↑ ↑	

COURSE 2. HOW TO MAKE BAD HABITS
BREAK THEMSELVES

1001. Habit is a most important part of mind power and mind organization. The breaking of bad habits and the acquiring of good h___s can be controlled.		habits
1002. The right, or good, h__t is a boon and a friend. Acquiring good habits will surely help you form the habit of happiness and success.		habit
1003. The good habit is a blessing, but the bad ____ is your worst enemy.		habit
1004. Good habits are wonderful time-savers. Things that would ordinarily take effort and concentration are done automatically if they are habitual. A ____ habit is a time-saver.		good
1005. A ___ habit is a vice, a despotical master. A bad habit is time consuming, annoying (to others as well as to you) and an implacable enemy.		bad
1006. Habits can be controlled, and I intend to teach you how in this programed learning course. If you answer all the questions and do the things I tell you to do, you will learn to c____l your habits.		control
1007. Let's take it a step at a time. You want to learn to get rid of bad habits and also to acquire ____ habits.		good
1008. It is easy to fall into the trap of bad h___s, but quite another matter to break them.		habits
1009. Of course, many authorities suggest that you break any bad habit by an act of will; simply stopping the h___.		habit

117

1010. This, of course, is the result you're after, but not necessarily the way of attaining it. If you could simply ____ a bad habit by wanting to, there'd be no problem.		break
1011. Of course, although that in itself won't necessarily do it, you must really want to b___ that ____ in order to start wearing it down (and out).		break habit
1012. No, I don't believe you can directly attack the habit itself. You have to get a bit sneaky here and attack that ____ circuitously.		habit
1013. In the following frames, I'll discuss six or seven sneak attacks. Each or all of them will be helpful in breaking your ___ habits.		bad
1014. Do keep in mind that it all depends on the habit you want to get rid of, and just how ingrained that ____ is.		habit
1015. I can only make suggestions. Which of the methods will fit or work for you personally, is an individual thing. Let's start by assuming that you really w___ to break that habit, whatever it is!		want
1016. For some simple bad habits, the system of repetition will help. The system of r_____n means to consciously repeat the bad habit!		repetition
1017. You see, bad h___s are subconscious and automatic actions of the will. Making the action a c_____s one and bringing it out in the open – can help.		habits conscious
1018. Some habits are easily broken once they are brought out of the realm of the subconscious. Let me give you just one example of this rep___tion method.		repetition

1019. Say you're learning to type and you've been hitting the wrong key each time you want to type an e. You actually practice or r___t consciously hitting that wrong key for a while.		repeat
1020. After some work at this, you'll find that you can now consciously and deliberately hit the right key. This is the r___tion method of breaking a simple bad habit.		repetition
1021. Of course, in some cases, this would be asinine. If you wanted to break your smoking habit, it certainly wouldn't be wise to r___t it or practice it!		repeat
1022. But the r___tion method can help with simple physical bad habits, as in the typing example.		repetition
1023. Let's assume, however, that you are a slave to the bad habit of fingernail biting. You really would like to b___k that habit.		break
1024. Here are seven different sneak attacks that you might launch. One or more of them, if used consistently for a while, will be of great help in wearing down that h___.		habit
1025. First, the 'delay' method. Assuming you bite your nails at certain times habitually, you must break that time-hold. It must be thrown off kilter, or off schedule. So, use the d___y method.		delay
1026. Think about it. Do you bite your nails when you're particularly tense? Well, just once, consciously, during a tense moment, don't do it! D___y it! You'll bite like crazy when that moment is over.		Delay
1027. Do you smoke a cigarette about once every half hour? Well, if you want to break that habit, d___ it consciously for a while.		delay

1028. Break the pattern of your habit by the _____ method.		delay
1029. Do you bite your nails whenever you're about to call on a customer? Well, right now, start d____ing it. Just for your next call, don't do it! Do it after you see him, not before.		delaying
1030. This is one way of breaking part of the h____ pattern. Bad habits must be attacked gradually, on one or more fronts.		habit
1031. Similar to the delay method is the 'time-clock' method. You'll interfere, or throw off kilter, that ingrained h____ if you force yourself to indulge at certain times only.		habit
1032. Set any time for it. Say to yourself that you'll b____ your fingernails down to the knuckles every hour on the h__r, but not in between.		bite hour
1033. Remember that the object is not to turn you into a clock watcher or to make you breathlessly await the proper time, but simply to throw the h____ off the track; off kilter.		habit
1034. It's bringing that subconscious action out into the open where you can see it and attack it. It's making it a c_____s action instead of a subconscious one.		conscious
1035. The 'coffee break' method. Set aside certain periods of time during the day when you will not bite your nails under any circumstances. You'll take a b___k from your habit during those times.		break
1036. This serves two purposes. Again, it is interfering, or throwing the habit or routine off k____r.		kilter

1037. And, just as important, you are asserting your will power. You are deliberately and consciously taking a premeditated step to b___k that habit!		break
1038. I just mentioned will power. Of course, the more will power you possess, the easier it will be for you to break any habit. Later on, I will teach you how to strengthen your will p____.		power
1039. After you get through the will power section, you might come back here and see how much easier it will be for you to apply these methods for b_____g bad habits and acquiring good ones.		breaking
1040. For the time being, I suggest that you continue to try these methods. Launch these s___k attacks against your bad ____s and start to see some improvement and results immediately.		sneak habits
1041. The 'disturbance' method. Change the usual pattern of your habit by setting up interferences and dis_____s.		disturbances
1042. For example, if you enjoy biting your nails sitting down, insist to yourself that you'll only do it st____g up from now on.		standing
1043. If you're in the habit of biting your thumbnail only, start to consciously bite your forefinger n___ instead of the thumbnail.		nail
1044. If you're accustomed to one brand of cigarette, change it! Get some that are milder, stronger, unfiltered, etc. You're consciously ch____g the pattern of your habit.		changing
1045. The smooth subconscious continuity of your habit is being interfered with; you're c_____ly throwing it off kilter.		consciously

121

1046. Consciously introduce as much confusion or dis_____ce to the routine as you possibly can.		disturbance
1047. The 'twenty-four hour' methòd. Simply make up your mind to avoid your bad habit for just <u>one</u> full day. That's all. Just o__ full day.		one
1048. This is a drastic frontal attack. If done properly and with will power, it can break your bad _____ in one fell swoop.		habit
1049. Alcoholics Anonymous has a twenty-four h___ club. The members stay off liquor for only <u>one</u> day at a time.		hour
1050. Thinking about giving something up forever can present a frightening picture. But thinking of giving up anything for just ___ day is a bit easier to bear.		one
1051. You must talk yourself into this. "I'll bite all my nails off tomorrow, but just for t___y, I won't do it at all."		today
1052. Of course, the next day you do the same thing! Talk to yourself. "I've done this for one day, certainly I'm man enough to do it for just ___ more day! Tomorrow I'll make up for it, etc."		one
1053. And so on. After enough time has elapsed, the urge to indulge in the h____ is gone; or arrested, anyway.		habit
1054. Then there's the 'challenge' method. Challenge yourself; make a mental wager that you will not indulge in the h____ any more.		habit

122

1055. The best way is to tell your close friends about it. Invite them to help you to toe the line, to deride you, laugh at you if necessary, if you indulge in the _____ again.		habit
056. In this way, you're forcing yourself against wall. Again, a drastic all-out attack. Look at it rith good humor, make a game of it. Ch_____ ourself!		Challenge
1057. Finally, the 'substitution' method. Try substituting a good habit for a bad one. Erasmus said, "A nail is driven out by another nail; habit is overcome by habit." So try to s_____e another habit for the one you wish to break.		substitute
1058. Every time you feel like biting your fingernails, get involved in some project you've been putting off for too long. When you feel the need for a cigarette, s_____e a piece of gum or candy, and so on.		substitute
1059. Once more, you are consciously breaking the pattern or continuity of your bad habit. You are c_____ly interfering with it.		consciously
1060. Try these methods! No, it isn't easy. Why should it be? It can't be easy to curtail a h____that you've been a slave to for years or almost all of your life.		habit
1061. If you indulge your habit at different (from usual) times, or avoid indulging at definite times as you always have before, you're using the d___y method of attack.		delay
1062. If you set a definite time only in which to indulge your bad habit, you're using the time-c__k method.		clock
1063. If you set aside certain periods during the day in which you will not indulge under any circumstances, you're applying the coffee-_____ method.		break

1064. If you change the usual pattern of your habit.. If you interfere with it, make it less enjoyable, you're using the dis_____e method.		disturbance
1065. If you decide to stop indulging your bad habit for just one day at a time, you're using the twenty-four h___ method.		hour
1066. If you make a wager with yourself that you will not indulge, and if you ask your friends to deride you if you do, you're applying the ch_____e method.		challenge
1067. If you do something, anything, else at the moment that you'd rather indulge in your habit, you're using the s_____n method.		substitution
1068. Remember that you can use one or more, or all of these to fight any particular h___. Not only the ones I've used as examples.		habit.
1069. For instance, the twenty-four hour and the challenge methods go very well together. Challenge yourself to give up the habit for just the ___ day. Tell your friends about it, etc.		one
1070. Use the delay and the disturbance methods together. You can even throw the time-clock method in there. Use all the ammunition you want or need to beat that h___!		habit
1071. I've given quite a bit of space to getting rid of bad habits. How about acquiring good ones? A g___d habit can be a faithful friend through life.		good
1072. And you can acquire them. The key to acquiring good habits is concentration and attention. Do anything with att_____ long enough and it must become a habit.		attention

1073. If you find it difficult to do anything the same way twice, you're doing it without a_____n.		attention
1074. You can make anything a habit if you do it, at first, consistently and with conscious a_____.		attention
1075. Do you usually forget to lock your door when you leave? Would you like to create the habit of always, without fail, l___ing that door?		locking
1076. Force yourself, at first, to think of it. Do it with thought and c_____ attention for a while, and before you know it, it will be a habit.		conscious
1077. Start to think about it as you're getting dressed and ready to leave. In a surprisingly short while, you'll be locking that door automatically and without thinking. Then it's a h___!		habit
1078. These tips may be a little easier said than done at first. So here are a few suggestions to lead you along slowly. Answer the questions, but more important, try the suggestions. If you don't ___ them, they're of little use.		try
1079. Define the habit you wish to form, in detail. Know just what it's supposed to do for you, and allow it to get started properly. D_____e the habit you wish to form.		Define
1080. Start out by def___g the habit and making a voiced, or preferably written pledge. This pl___ will serve as a reminder to work at, and form, that new habit.		defining pledge
1081. Start to do the thing you want to become habit at the time, or circumstance, where you want it to work. Just practicing the h___ any time is worthless. Practice it at the proper t___.		habit time

1082. The time to start practicing the action of always locking your door is when you leave the house; not just any time. Practice the habit at the p_____ time.		proper
1083. Once you've de____d the action and have started doing it at the p____r time, set up a definite way or method of action. At first, do it that way all the time. Make the manner or method of action in-violable. Do it the same way all the time.		defined proper
1084. Do not differ in any way from the original action, or that di_____e will become a part of your new habit.		difference
1085. Most important, be consistent. If at first you repeat the action in the same way, at the same time and in the same manner – it will soon become automatic, and your new h____has asserted itself.		habit
1086. I must stress the importance of acquiring the h__t of acquiring good new habits. This can be one of the most useful assets through life.		habit
1087. Most successful people have found more time for everything, including creative thinking, because they've trained themselves to let h___ take care of all the small, necessary, repetitive chores.		habit
1088. Even unhappiness, very often, is nothing more than a bad habit! Why not work at acquiring the good habit of h____ss?		happiness
1089. If you wake up grouchy most mornings, get into the habit of looking in the mirror and smiling at yourself! Sounds idiotic, I know, but try it and surprise yourself. H_____ss can become a habit!		Happiness
1090. The habit of smiling is an asset in more ways than one. And, it is a habit! People will like you more, and you'll avoid unpleasant situations. It's difficult to argue with someone who is sincerely sm___ng at you.		smiling

1091. Most of the good and the bad, the faults and virtues, in our personalities are nothing but h___. Making prompt decisions is a good h_____ which can save countless hours and much unhappiness and it can be acquired.		habit habit
1092. Being shy is usually only an uncomfortably bad habit. It can be overcome by replacing it with the g___ habit of being interested in others and thinking of them and their comfort.		good
1093. But I don't need to list them all. I do want to stress upon you that you can acquire g__ h___ s and break the bad ones with the methods taught to you here. Let's review how to form good habits once again:		good habits
1094. Define the habit you wish to form. Lay out a plan so that you know exactly what the habit is supposed to do for you. D____ the habit.		Define
1095. After defining the habit, make a conscious pledge to do it. This will serve as a reminder. After defining the habit, make a p_____ to do it.		pledge
1096. Practice the action at the proper time. After defining it, and making a mental or written pledge, be sure to do it and practice it at the _____ time.		proper
1097. Set up definite ways and methods of action. Do it exactly the s___ way all the time.		same
1098. Do not deviate in any way from the original action. If you do, that deviation will become part of the habit. Do not d_____ from the action that you wish to become habit.		deviate
1099. Be consistent! Consistency is habit! Don't just practice the action every other time; practice it c_____tly.		consistently

1100. Most important, do the actions, at first, with <u>attention</u>. They will not become habit if you don't do them, at first, with conscious thought and a _____ .		attention
1101. And finally, I cannot stress enough the importance of <u>trying</u> the methods I've taught you here. Both for breaking ___ habits and acquiring ____ ones, you must t___ my methods.		bad good try
1102. This, of course, holds true for anything and everything you'll be learning in this course. Just reading passively is a waste of time. You <u>must</u> actively <u>try</u> my methods. Be sure to ___ the methods!		try
1103. You certainly have nothing to lose by trying them, and everything to gain! So, I leave the subject of habit, stressing again that you must actually and actively use and ___ my systems!!		try
You have now completed Course #2 of Harry Lorayne's <u>Instant Mind Power</u> Teaching-Machine. Course #3 Begins on the next sheet.	No answer required.	
	↑ ↑	
COURSE 3: HOW TO BUILD A WILL OF IRON 1104. The discussion of habits is a natural lead-in to the subject of will power as well as some of the other subjects I'll be teaching you. If you've tried (see next frame)	No answer required.	
1104. (continued) some of my methods for breaking bad habits and acquiring good ones, you've been using will _____ .		power
1105. As a matter of fact, they are so closely related that some of the rules for breaking and acquiring habits hold true for strengthening your ____ power.		will

1106. You can do anything in life you want to if you only have the will power to do it. How do you go about strengthening that w___ p____? Well, start by reading and studying the following frames. Try the systems and suggestions.		will power
1107. Answer all the questions and <u>do</u> what I tell you to. Remember, it is always important for you to do and t__ the systems.		try
1108. I will teach you certain rules, or steps, to follow. No one rule is sufficient by itself, to s_____n your will power. You must use them all.		strengthen
1109. And, the rules must be used in the proper order. Of course, that will be obvious to you, since one rule will naturally follow the other, like the links of a ch___.		chain
1110. To s_____n your will power, you must learn and apply <u>all</u> of the rules.		strengthen
1111. The first rule is:- <u>Be Sure You Really Want It Badly Enough!</u> It is difficult to apply or practice will _____ on some vague and ephemeral desire.		power
1112. If you think, "Some day I'd like to learn that;" forget it! You probably never will. You don't w___ it badly enough.		want
1113. Even if you think, "Gosh, I wish I could do that;" that's not wanting it badly enough either. Anything you want to do or learn b__ly enough, you can do or learn.		badly
1114. Unfortunately, wishing will <u>not</u> make it so! You must, first and foremost, learn the difference between the wish and the <u>will</u> to do or learn anything. W___ing will not make it so.		Wishing

1115. Do you see the difference between, "I wish I could learn to do that" and "I will learn to do that"? Change 'wish' to 'w__' and you're on your way to strengthening your will power.		will
1116. Any time you change your thought "I would like to; I ought to; I wish I could" to "I will," you are applying my first rule. You want it b__ly enough.		badly
1117. Part and parcel of this first rule is to sit down and mentally discuss with yourself why you want to do or learn any particular thing badly e_____.		enough
1118. It will help if you pinpoint your reasons for wanting it. Tell yourself w__ you want to do or learn this thing.		why
1119. It's usually a good idea to also list the importance of each reason. They go hand in hand, of course. Tell yourself why you want to do or learn the particular thing, and the im_____ of each reason.		importance
1120. This mental, or written, conversation with yourself will help you apply the first rule. Pinpointing the reasons for wanting it and listing the importance of each r____n has made you feel sure that you really want to attain this accomplishment b____ e____gh.		reason badly enough
1121. Say you've finally decided that you really want to learn to drive. 'Rap' in that desire. Pinpoint all the r_____s; there must be many. Now beside each reason, list its im_____.		reasons importance
1122. Now you've 'rapped' in that desire; you really want to learn to drive badly enough. You've gone through the trouble of pinpointing and listing and you've taken your first step toward strengthening your w__ p___.		will power
1123. You must _____ the reasons for wanting to do, or learn, any particular thing. a) accept b) love c) pinpoint d) ignore		c) pinpoint

1124. After pinpointing your reasons, list the _____ of each one. a) importance b) size c) growth d) spelling		a) importance
1125. These are sub-rules to help you apply this main rule; Be Sure You _____ Want It Badly Enough. a) Don't b) Might c) Won't d) Really		d) Really
1126. So remember, the first rule for strengthening your will power is:- <u>Be Sure You Really Want It</u> B____ E____.		Badly Enough
1127. The next rule is:- <u>Have Confidence That You Can Do It!</u> If you have to, really <u>force</u> yourself to believe you ___ do it.		can
1128. And you really can, you know! Don't let anyone (especially yourself) tell you different. You c__ do <u>anything</u> you really w___ to.		can want
1129. Look at it this way: Even if you don't achieve mastery, or perfection, in the thing you want to accomplish, you will still do it better, or have more knowledge of it, than you do at this moment. You must have confidence that you c__ do it.		can
1130. Maybe you've often said, "Gee, I wish I knew something about art." Well, change that to, "I <u>will</u> learn something about art," apply rule #1; then have c_____ce that you will.		confidence
1131. You may not become a connoisseur, but you will eventually know more about art than you do now. You've taken your first two s___s toward that goal.		steps
1132. Many of us are stopped in our tracks at this point because memories of past failures drain our c_____ce.		confidence

1133. Remember this: Past failure is no reason for not believing in present success! You must be aware that most of our great inventions and a - quisitions of knowledge were realized in spite of, and most often, because of past f____s.		failures
1134. Okay, so you'll make mistakes. So what! If you never make m____s you'll never achieve or accomplish anything!		mistakes
1135. I'll be discussing fear of f____e much more thoroughly in the section on how to control your worry and fear.		failure
1136. In the meantime, just make yourself believe (because it's true) that surmounting obstacles and making m____s is part of accomplishing anything.		mistakes
1137. Be like the man who was asked if he could play the piano - and replied, "I don't know; I never tried!" Have c_____ce that you can do it, or certainly try.		confidence
1138. Stop thinking, "I don't think so; I haven't the time; I failed before; etc." Let your battle cry, or motto, be, "Of course I can do it!" Do this, and you've taken two giant steps toward strengthening your w___ p___.		will power
1139. The third, and probably the most important, rule is:- BEGIN. That's it and that's all - just begin. Nothing and no one, no power on earth can ever s_____en your will power if you don't b___n.		strengthen begin

1140. In order to accomplish or learn anything, we must, above all, simply
    a) forget it
    b) begin
    c) cry
    d) confide in others
		b) begin

1141. Again, let me give you some sub-rules to help you apply the main rule. The main rule is simply to b___.		begin

1142. Don't look at the over-all task of any accomplishment right away. It may loom too vast, too much for you to handle. This can drain your c_____ce and keep you from beginning.		confidence
1143. Instead think of it this way: Any large task is made up of many smaller, simpler tasks. Take it one step at a time. All you need think about is that first s___.		step
1144. The longest walk is made up of many small steps. And you'll never get to your goal unless you take the first one. Look at the thing you desire one s___ at a time.		step
1145. Sure, I'm throwing a few clichés at you, but a cliché becomes a cliché because it's <u>true</u>! And what's the difference, so long as it helps to strengthen your w___ p___.		will power
1146. Okay, take that first ____ and you've <u>begun</u>!		step
1147. I'll give you another cliché: "He has half the deed done who has made a beginning!" The ____ step is your beginning.		first
1148. Another sub-rule: - Keep your final goal in mind! Never mind the vast, unsurmountable task ahead, but keep your eye on the final g___.		goal
1149. This is your incentive. Without a visible (mental) goal, there is no motivation. So think of that eventual g___.		goal
1150. Many people I've spoken to have rarely begun because their attitude was, "Oh come on, it'll take years to learn (or do) that." The g____ was vague in their minds.		goal

1151. Remember this:- If it takes five years to learn or accomplish something <u>now</u>, it will take five years from <u>whenever</u> you begin! So you might as well b____ <u>now</u>.		begin
1152. So, although I do want you to keep your goal in mind, I also want you to consider the accomplishment one s___ at a time.		step
1153. Don't try to plan out the entire thing. Plan one step at a time; plan for the next few minutes, the next hour, the next day, etc. And once you've begun, keep doing that next step at a ____.		time
1154. Write one sentence at a time and you'll eventually write a book. Take one step at a time and you'll eventually walk the longest journey. Save one dollar at a time and you'll eventually have a significant bank account. Just think of taking one ____ at a time.		step
1155. Get through with that one step, and the feeling of accomplishment that comes with it will be an added incentive to go on to the next ____.		step
1156. Each feeling of accomplishment, each added incentive, will add a bit more strength to your w___ p____.		will power
1157. Okay; if you apply, and think of, all the things I've taught you, it will help you to apply the third main, and important, rule: B____. Apply it, and you've added another inch to that w__ p____ bicep.		Begin will power
1158. The <u>first</u> rule for strengthening your will power is: Be sure you really ____ it badly enough.		want
1159. The second rule for strengthening your will power is: Have c_____ that you can do it.		confidence

1160. The third rule for strengthening your will power is: B____.		Begin
1161. The next rule to help you strengthen your w___ p____, and to help you accomplish anything, is: <u>Back Yourself Into A Corner Occasionally.</u>		will power
1162. Being backed into a corner has been the inspiration for many accomplishments. If you can manage to purposely b___ yourself into a corner, it will work just as <u>necessity</u> does.		back
1163. All this means is that you should purposely make it hard for yourself occasionally. There are many ways of doing this. One is to set a dead-line for doing something. Set a ____-line.		dead
1164. If you set a dead-line and make up your mind that you must meet it, no ifs, ands or buts, you're backing yourself into a c____r.		corner
1165. As I taught you in the section on habits, tell your friends about something you intend to accomplish by a certain time. Invite them to deride you if you fail to do so. You're backing yourself into a _____.		corner
1166. Even though the kidding you'll get will be good-natured, you'll still want to avoid it. It will force you to do what you said you would. You're b___ing yourself into a corner.		backing
1167. Tell your spouse about it. Set things up so that if you don't do or accomplish what you say you will, you'll be a lesser person in his or her eyes. You've really backed y____f into a tight corner.		yourself
1168. Put yourself on the spot by exposing yourself to temptation. If you've just given up smoking, keep a pack of cigarettes handy. Each time you avoid the temptation, you've taken one more s____ forward.		step

135

1169. As per the rule for breaking bad habits, challenge yourself. Make a mental wager with yourself that you will do a certain thing at a certain time. Deride yourself, force yourself to take that next ___ .		step
1170. All right. You have some sub-rules for backing yourself into a corner. One way is to set a d___-___ .		dead-line
1171. Another way is to put yourself on the spot by exposing yourself to t_____ n .		temptation
1172. Or, you can make mental wagers with yourself, or set up ch_____ s.		challenges
1173. These are all aids for applying the fourth rule to help you strengthen your will power. Back yourself into a _____ occasionally.		corner
1174. You needn't be concerned about backing yourself into that corner. Take my word for it, you'll do whatever it is you have to do. Then you'll be ready to take care of the ___ step.		next
1175. Don't let discouragement stop you. In most instances, achievement is just around the corner from discouragement. So don't be deterred by d_____ment.		discouragement
1176. Take care of that particular phase; that particular duty or chore; get over the hump, and get to the next ___ .		step
1177. The fifth and final rule for strengthening your w___ p____ , and accomplishing anything you wish to accomplish is: Form The Habit.		will power

1178. I don't have to go into detail on this, I'm sure, since I've already taught you about h____s.		habits
1179. And I've told you before that w___ p_____ and h____ go hand in hand.		will power habit
1180. It's worth a frame or two here, however, just to remind you that after you've done anything once, it's easier the next time. Do it again, and it becomes still e___r.		easier
1181. Once you've applied my rules for strengthening your will power to any one project, they will be easier to apply to the n__t one.		next
1182. And so on, until you've made, or formed, the h____ of will power.		habit
1183. So I must be repetitive here, and stress again that you must actually use and apply these rules. Do so and you'll be strengthening your w___ p____ and the habit of will power.		will power
1184. The challenge idea, as mentioned in the section on habits and here, is one which comes in handy in many ways. If you want to make unpleasant duties and chores much more pleasant to accomplish, use the ch_____ idea.		challenge
1185. Make every unpleasant chore a ch_____. Make a game out of it.		challenge
1186. Making a difficult and unpleasant job into a ch_____ and a game not only makes it easier, but will give you a much greater feeling of accomplishment.		challenge

1187. Finally, always keep this in mind:- Thoughts <u>must</u> lead to <u>action</u>. All the thinking in the world will accomplish nothing, if it doesn't eventually lead to a_____.		action
1188. Thinking without a_____ is really, in most cases, nothing more than day-dreaming. And day-dreaming, unless it in itself leads to action, will get you nowhere!		action
1189. Let me remind you of another cliche: Do it now!! Any time you get a good thought, or a strong desire to learn or accomplish something, act on it <u>immediately</u>. Take at least the first s__p.		step
1190. That good thought, or desire, will evaporate if it is not acted on im_____.		immediately
1191. So, form the <u>habit</u> of taking at least the first step whenever a good th_____ or desire comes to you.		thought
1192. Each and every time a good thought or desire evaporates because of inappropriate action, or no a____ at all, you've drained or lost a bit of that new-found will power.		action
1193. That, incidentally, is one of the basic ideas behind this form of learning, the programed l_____ng course.		learning
1194. I am forcing you to <u>act</u> with each frame. You must answer each and every question. You're <u>doing</u> something! Each time you pick up your pencil to answer a question, I am forcing you to ___.		act
1195. So; thought leads to action; and _____ leads to achievement.		action

1196. Now before leaving the subject of w___ p___ and accomplishing what you want, here's a final review.		will power
1197. There are five main rules to apply in order to strengthen your will power. The first one is: Be sure you ____ it badly enough.		want
1198. You must change the <u>wish</u> to do or learn something to the ____ to do or learn it.		will
1199. To help you apply this rule, it will help to pinpoint the r___s, and the <u>importance</u> of the reasons for wanting to do, or learn it.		reasons

1200. This will aid you in '_____' in that desire or will.
    a) believing
    b) giving
    c) subduing
    d) rapping
		d) rapping

1201. The second rule is: Have _____ that you can do it.		confidence
1202. Do not let past failures drain your c_____ .		confidence
1203. Let your battle cry be, "Of course I ___ do it."		can
1204. The third and most important rule is contained in one word: ____ .		Begin.

1205. Take every large task one step at a time. But above all, take that first ___.		step
1206. At the same time, try to keep your eye on the final ___. This will furnish the incentive.		goal
1207. The fourth rule is: Back yourself into a _____ occasionally.		corner
1208. Set a ___ - __ for anything you wish to accomplish.		dead-line
1209. Tell your friends about it. Set things up in such a way that they will deride you if you don't do it. Set up ch_____s for yourself.		challenges
1210. Put yourself on the spot by exposing yourself to tem_____n.		temptation
1211. Don't let discouragement deter you. Achievement is usually just around the corner of dis_____t.		discouragement
1212. The fifth rule is: Form the _____.		Habit.
1213. Habit and w__ p___ go hand in hand.		will power

1214. Form the _____ of will power.		habit
1215. Use the ch_____ idea to make difficult and unpleasant duties and chores easier to do.		challenge
1216. Make it a habit to always have your thought or desire lead to a) action b) police headquarters c) water d) wishing		a) action
1217. Thinking without action is usually nothing more than day-_____.		dreaming
1218. As soon as you get the thought or desire, act on the first s___ immediately or it will start to evaporate.		step
1219. Finally, and with purposeful repetition, I must tell you again to try these rules. If you do not apply and use them they cannot possibly help to strengthen your w__ p____ .		will power
1220. You must a____ these rules in order for them to help you!		apply
You have now completed Course #3 of Harry Lorayne's Instant Mind Power Teaching-Machine. Course #4 Begins on the next sheet.		

COURSE #4: HOW TO OVERCOME WORRY AND FEAR		
1221. Part of mind power and mind organization is the ability to control needless worry and fear. The important word here is n_____ss.		needless
1222. It is natural and normal to have doubts and uncertainties. Particularly in this hectic age we live in. It is natural to worry. W___y is a normal mental reaction.		Worry
1223. We all w___y occasionally. And in most cases, that's good. Worry can be the stepping-stone to action.		worry
1224. If you're worried about something, and that w____ forces you to do something about it; that's fine.		worry
1225. Worry is thought, and if the th_____ leads to action and/or accomplishment, then your worry is serving a purpose.		thought
1226. It's when your worrying becomes chronic or habitual - without leading to a_____n that you may be harming yourself.		action
1227. If your w_____s and fears are causing you to be unhappy, something must be done about it.		worries
1228. If you've learned how to control habits and your w___ p_____ , you should have no trouble controlling worry and fear.		will power
1229. Let me try to help in my own way. First; what exactly is w____? Well, there's no doubt that it can be one of your worst enemies.		worry

1230. Usually worries are nothing but figments of your imagination. If you never worried at all, it would show a lack of im_____ .		imagination
1231. Essentially, _____ is a fear reaction over a future event which may never materialize. You're paying interest on your troubles before that interest is due!		worry
1232. All right then, if you fret and stew over every little thing; if you're always doubtful and uncertain for no apparent reason; if you're letting anxieties and apprehensions get the upper hand; if you're an hab____l worrier; I think I can be of some help.		habitual
1233. The first thing to do is to make yourself believe that most of the things you worry about, seldom (or never) happen! Here's how you can prove to yourself that most of them seldom h_____.		happen
1234. Right now try to remember the things you were worrying about a year ago! Can you remember any of them? And if you do, did they ever h____?		happen
1235. And if you're attributing this to a bad memory, why not take a moment right now and list all the things you're w_____d about at this moment?		worried
1236. Go ahead; do it. It will be time well spent. It will prove that most of the things you worry about just never h_____ or materialize.		happen
1237. And if they do h_____, they're seldom as bad as you think they'll be.		happen
1238. Place this list of worries in a safe place, and check it six months or a year from now. This alone will prove the folly of w___y.		worry

1239. You've just been given your first rule for controlling worry. Make yourself believe ('cause it's true) that most of the things you worry about seldom h____.		happen
1240. Another tip; Look within yourself and make sure you're not the martyr type of worrier!	No answer required.	
1241. Sometimes our worries are nothing more than disguised attempts to gain sympathy and attention! This is dangerous and can cause habitual worry. Be sure you're not the m____r type of worrier.		martyr
1242. You'll have to really look within yourself to check this. It could be a subconscious reaction. But if you think about it a while, you'll know whether you're the m____r type of worrier or not.		martyr
1243. In most cases, the worry itself is more agonizing and painful than whatever it is you're w____d about.		worried
1244. Minor frustrations, failures and annoyances should be anticipated, not worried about. Since they are inevitable, expect and an____te them and you'll have no need to worry about them.		anticipate
1245. I'm sure I don't have to stress this. We all know that life is abundant with these minor failures, troubles, frustrations, annoyances, etc. Accept them; overcome them; an____te them, and you've eliminated a large slice of worry.		anticipate
1246. It is even possible and beneficial to look forward to some of these minor frustrations! Look at them as challenges; and you've eliminated w___.		worry
1247. Since these minor frustrations are inevitable, doesn't it make sense to anticipate them and to consider them ch____s?		challenges

144

1248. I think you'll find that if you can make this a habit, you'll eventually <u>welcome</u> these minor fr_____ns.		frustrations
1249. You'll accept them as challenges and get a kick' out of overcoming them. If you do a_____t them as c_____s, you have no time or need to worry about them.		accept challenges
1250. Learn to accept the inevitable! This doesn't mean to feel that there's nothing you can do about anything. But, for minor frustrations and annoyances, make a habit of accepting the in_____.		inevitable
1251. Let's face it, there isn't much you can do about it when it's snowing except wear boots. There isn't much you can do about a tooth that must come out, except get it out! Learn to accept the in_____.		inevitable
1252. If you inwardly enjoy worrying because it brings you attention and sympathy, you're the _____ type of worrier. a) good b) bad c) martyr d) master		c) martyr
1253. If you list everything you're worried about right now, and check that list a year from now, you'll prove to yourself that most of the things seldom h_____.		happen
1254. And if they did happen, they weren't any-where as bad as you th____t they'd be.		thought
1255. If you learn to accept the in_____, most of your worries will disappear.		inevitable
1256. Now, here's my favorite method of eliminating worry. Whenever something comes up which may cause w____, think of the <u>worst</u> that can possibly happen!		worry

1257. Think of the w___ that can happen, and assuming it does, is it a matter of life and death, or the end of the world?		worst
1258. If it isn't a matter of life and death or the end of the world, simply prepare for, or assume that, the w____ will happen – then forget about it!		worst
1259. For example, did you recently make an investment which you're worried about? The worst that can happen is, you'll lose the entire in__ - ___. Will that break you? Will it ruin your life?		investment
1260. If not, assume that it's all lost; accept this and what is there to w____ about now?		worry
1261. Of course, the odds are you won't lose the entire investment. If you only lose a small part of it, or if you make money, you'll be pleasantly surprised and you haven't wasted time w____ing about it.		worrying
1262. If you do lose the total amount, well, assuming you couldn't have done anything to salvage it, like getting out with a lesser loss, etc., at least you haven't worried needlessly. You already prepared for the _____ that could happen.		worst
1263. Are you w____d about losing your job? Have you done everything you can to avoid this eventuality?		worried
1264. If you have, prepare for the w____. You are going to lose your job.		worst
1265. So – do what you would do if you actually lost it! Look around for other job opportunities; think about it; prepare for the worst; then __ something about it.		do

1266. Whether or not you lose your job is immaterial for this discussion. What is important is, you've accepted and/or prepared for the w____ that could happen and you haven't worried excessively about it. Instead, you've d__e something about it.		worst done
1267. Hand in hand with accepting the w____ that can happen, is preparing for minor dilemmas and worries.		worst
1268. I'm referring to the really minor w____s which are most often caused by our own laziness and procrastination.		worries
1269. Let's get these really m___r worries out of the way. If you're going to worry, you may as well worry about the big things!		minor
1270. Are you constantly worried about being iate? P___re for it by cultivating the habit of always leaving a bit earlier. Why worry about it?		Prepare
1271. Are you constantly worried about getting lost? D_ something about it! Get good maps of the areas you're driving in, spend a little time learning how to read those maps. Why w____ about it?		Do worry
1272. One or two of your tires are nearly bald and you're worrying about flats? Get new tires right now. You'll have to soon anyway; why w____ about it?		worry
1273. All these really silly m___r worries are caused by your own laziness and procrastination.		minor
1274. The simple solution is to d_ something about them immediately, and the w____ is eliminated.		do worry

1275. Stop procrastinating; d_ something and half your m___r worries are over.		do minor
1276. Are you worried about more important things, like your health? Do s_____g about it. See your doctor for a check-up; let him w____ about it!		something worry worry
1277. Are you worried about the condition of your teeth? Have them checked now. Do something a____ it; why worry?		about
1278. Are you worried that you're smoking too much? Apply all the rules for breaking bad h____s that you learned before. Do something about it. B___k that habit!		habits Break
1279. Make it a habit to pre___e for and do something about minor, and not so minor, worries.		prepare
1280. This also holds true for worries which must be considered of greater importance. But are these the type of worries which cover up guilt feelings? Be sure your worries are not cover-ups for g_____ feelings.		guilt
1281. For example: Are you worried about what would happen to your family if something happened to you? Is this a g__t worry because you've neglected to insure yourself properly?		guilt
1282. Then check your insurance coverage; make sure your family is well protected, and stop feeling g___y and worrying about it!		guilty
1283. Are you worried about the physical safety of your family? Have you done everything possible to insure that safety? If so, there's no reason for g__t or w___y.		guilt worry

148

1284. You've done something about it; now forget it and s__p w____ing.		stop worrying
1285. Another good rule is to <u>belittle</u> the importance of what you're worrying about. Minimize its effect by ridiculing and disparaging the im_____ of it.		importance
1286. Cultivate a "so what" attitude. The minor frustrations and annoyances of life cannot really hurt you if you don't allow them to. Shrug your shoulders, say "so ____," and forget it.		what
1287. Accept the inevitable! Learn to examine each worry separately. If you can change or modify the situation that's causing the worry, fine; do so. If not, apply some of the rules already taught you and then accept the _____.		inevitable
1288. This will work for minor and major worries. Are you worried about growing old? Why not prepare for, and a____t, the inevitable?		accept
1289. Why worry about growing older anyway; think of the alternative! Anyway, how do you know that ___ age isn't the most rewarding and finest part of life?		old
1290. I don't mean for you to sit and wait for old age; just stop worrying about it. Prepare for it? Sure. Work out a retirement or a pension plan, etc. But stop worrying ab___ it.		about
1291. You must train yourself to live with the things and conditions you cannot change. A____t them, and do the best you can under the circumstances.		Accept
1292. Such acceptance of the in_____ will relieve you of needless tension and prevent emotional disturbances.		inevitable

1293. All these rules and hints I've given you so far will help eliminate worry, if you apply them. Also apply some of the rules I've given you for controlling habits and w__ p____.		will power
1294. Worry is a bad h___t which can be broken with the help of a bit of will power.		habit
1295. Okay, a few more simple rules for eliminating and b___king the worry habit. When-ever you find yourself worrying – smile.		breaking
1296. That's right; just smile! I don't mean an idiotic grin, I mean a genuine s___.		smile
1297. You see, it is impossible to think of two things at the same time. And, in order to s___, you must think of something pleasant.		smile
1298. Do that and you can't worry at that moment. Try it. S____, and your present, momentary worry will be dissipated.		Smile
1299. Call it the rule of 'comparison.' Each time you worry about something, think of any pleasant things that are going to happen today, and s___.		smile
1300. It is impossible to th___ of two things at one time. Train yourself to think of something pleasant and to smile whenever you catch yourself worrying.		think
1301. Train yourself to c___re the pleasant with whatever you're worried about.		compare

1302. This rule goes farther than is apparent at first glance. You cannot smile and be grouchy at the same time. If you leave no room for w___ in your thoughts, the worry will dissipate itself.		worry
1303. Most of us are worriers because we leave ourselves too much time to w___ .		worry
1304. The best way to overcome habitual w___ is to become more active; either mentally or physically, or both. Try becoming more interested in others and their worries. You won't have t__e for yours, then.		worry time
1305. When you feel a worry coming on, keep your mind and your hands busy. The w___ won't be able to get a foot-hold on you if you're busy.		worry
1306. Farmers are the least susceptible to nervousness and chronic worrying because they are usually occupied from morning to night. They have no t___ to worry!		time
1307. If you have too much time for worrying, get interested in another hobby, mental or physical; and learn to s___ when you catch yourself worrying!		smile
1308. Learn to rationalize away your worry. Think of all the reasons you can why this particular stress and w___ should not exist or bother you.		worry
1309. This r_____tion is one more weapon for weakening and dissipating your worries.		rationalization
1310. Train yourself to r_____ize your worries.		rationalize

151

1311. Each of these rules go hand in hand with each other. One either leads to, or helps you to apply, the other. Rationalizing your worry will help you to assume that 'so ___' attitude.		what

1312. Assuming the 'so what' attitude will help you to ____ instead of sneer.
   a) be grouchy
   b) smile
   c) drink
   d) cry
		b) smile

1313. Finally, use a variation of the twenty-four hour method for breaking bad h___s. Set aside one special day each week in which you'll do all your worrying!		habits
1314. That's right! Make up your mind that you will worry (about everything) on just that ___ special day.		one
1315. The other days can now be used in a care-free manner. Let the worries accumulate for that one special ___.		day
1316. When that day arrives, lock yourself away from everyone, and start w___ing. You may be surprised that most of the worries have become strangely vague and elusive.		worrying
1317. Some of them will have vanished without a trace! Try it! After spending that ___ special day worrying, go back to your worry-free existence until that day arrives again.		one
1318. You'll find the time you spend w___ing even on that one special day will be growing shorter and shorter!		worrying
1319. So - be sure you've d__e everything possible about any worrisome situation and are not worrying because of g___ feelings.		done guilt

1320. If the situation is beyond your control, learn to live with it. Accept the in_____.		inevitable
1321. Decide what is the w___t that can happen, accept and pr___e for that, and stop worrying about it.		worst prepare
1322. Make it a habit to prepare for minor worries. Do something about them; p_____ for them, and they are no longer worries.		prepare
1323. Train yourself to assume a 'so ___' attitude. Belittle your worries.		what
1324. Think of all the reasons why it's silly for a particular situation to worry you. Learn to _____ your worries. a) rationalize b) love c) hate d) recognize		a) rationalize
1325. Set aside___ special day in which to do all your worrying. Live the other days fully and in a worry-free, carefree manner.		one
## HOW TO THINK AWAY FEAR 1326. There isn't much to differentiate between w___ and fear. It's a case of the boil (worry) coming to a painful head (fear).		worry
1327. Rational anxiety or fear is an essential and useful part of living. F___, like pain, can be a warning of, a protection against, imminent danger.		Fear
1328. Fear of fire, fear of falling, and such, are basic and useful human fears. If you had no ___ of fire, sooner or later you'd be badly burned.		fear

1329. Fear can also be a good creative force. It was fear of ignorance that created schools; fear of food poisoning that created safer and healthier methods of food handling; f___ of accidents that created safety measures in all walks of life.		fear
1330. Knowledge brings awareness. So the more you know, the more there is to f___.		fear
1331. It is, however, irrational and unreasonable fears we must fight against. Most of the rules and ideas I gave you for eliminating w___ will also apply toward controlling or eliminating unreasonable fear.		worry
1332. Remember that for both w___ and f___, you must really want to get rid of them, or no rules or ideas in the world will help.		worry fear
1333. Assuming you really do ___ to get rid of unreasonable fears, my first and most important rule is Do The Thing You Fear!		want
1334. That's right! The best way to be rid of minor fears is to face up to them. Do the thing you f___.		fear
1335. Believe me when I tell you that many of the things you fear now can be faced squarely and even eventually enjoyed! F___ up to the things you fear.		Face
1336. Are you afraid of flying? Face up to it; d_ it once! See if there is something to be _____ of.		do afraid
1337. You may find that you really should be afraid of it. All right – then don't do it anymore. But you may conceivably find that there really is nothing to be _____ of. You may even enjoy it!		afraid

1338. Try the thing you f___ at least once! Even if it means sleeping in the dark; or flying; or petting a dog; or holding a cat; or making a decision and sticking to it.		fear
1339. Try it o__e – and at least see if you <u>should</u> be afraid of it.		once
1340. One of the simplest cures for minor fears I know is d__g the thing you fear. This deliberate act of f___g up to the fear, done intentionally and consciously several times in a row, will eventually eliminate the fear.		doing facing
1341. Remember, you'll never be victorious over a fear that is not brought out into the open so you can f___ it squarely.		face
1342. Another 'trick' or rule is to pretend or act as if your fear of any particular thing or situation simply didn't exist. Act as if, or pretend, that you are <u>not</u> a___.		afraid
1343. Pretend you're not afraid of a certain thing and you'll eventually cease <u>being a</u>____.		afraid
1344. These things must be formed into habits. You must f___e yourself, at first, to try, do, or face up to the <u>things</u> you ____.		force fear
1345. Force yourself, at first, to a__t unafraid, and before you know it, you <u>will be</u> un_____.		act unafraid
1346. Getting into more important, or major, fears. The most universal fear is the __ __ of death.		fear

1347. Here I can only remind you that it is silly to fear the inevitable. Remember to accept the in_____ .		inevitable
1348. There isn't a thing in the world you can do about it, so do your best to live with it. Try to minimize its effects on you as best you can; accept the in_____ , and forget about it.		inevitable
1349. Are you afraid of failure? Well, I've discussed this before. I can only tell you that those who are terrified of f_____ , usually are failures.		failure
1350. Being terrified of failure can only be instrumental in keeping you from trying. If you never t__ anything, you never accomplish anything, and you're a failure.		try
1351. Simply make up your mind that the real sign of success is not a straight, unmarked line to achievement, but the manner in which you overcome f_____ s!		failures
1352. Overcome your fear of failure by preparing an alternative, or saying, "so ____ ," and just go ahead and try.		what
1353. If your fear of failure makes you pr___e properly, and plan better, then that fear is helping you and not keeping you from trying.		prepare
1354. Although this gets back into the worry problem, I think that most of us are not frightened by the present. It's those imaginary, shadowy, future events that fill us with f___ .		fear
1355. Keep in mind that if you take care of the present, the future will take care of itself. Do the best you can now, and don't waste time fearing the f___ .		future

1356. Don't you realize that the more you dread tomorrow, the less time and inclination you'll have to face and enjoy today? Take care of the _____ and the future will take care of itself.		present
1357. Of course, you do all you can to insure a safer and happier tomorrow, but once you've done that, forget about it! Stop being a___d of life and you'll enjoy life.		afraid
1358. If you're a____d of serious illness, and it makes you go for health check-ups more often; that's good.		afraid
1359. But don't harbor unreasonable dreads. I think that more sickness is sometimes caused by the fear of disease than by the d_____ itself!		disease
1360. It's silly to stop living in order to live! If you're having your check-ups when you should; if you're doing what you can about anything, f___t about it.		forget
1361. As I said when discussing worry – prepare for things you fear whenever you can, then when there's nothing more you can do, forget about it. P_____ whenever you can.		Prepare
1362. It is always helpful to confide your fears to someone else. Don't bottle them up; talk them over with someone you can trust. Don't b____ up your fears and worries.		bottle
1363. T____g things out, brings them into the open and helps you to see the worry or f___ in a clearer light.		Talking fear
1364. This helps to apply the other rules of facing up to, and t____g the things you fear.		trying

1365. It will also help because usually you'll get advice on how to overcome the particular fear or how to lessen it. This is if you choose the right person to discuss it with. Choose someone you t___t and someone who perhaps knows more than you do.		trust
1366. Your doctor, clergyman, teacher, school counselor, etc., are good examples. D____ss your fears with someone you trust.		Discuss
1367. Finally, use the same idea I suggested for worry. Set aside one special d___ for the major fears.		day
1368. Use the same day that you're using for w_____ Just leave some of the time for your f___s.		worry fears
1369. The rest of the time, as long as you've done everything you can to p_____e for or eliminate the f___, be carefree and fear-free; forget about it!		prepare fear
1370. If you apply some, or all, of the rules, ideas, hints and suggestions I've given you, you'll be able to control your worries, and win the battle over your t____s.		fears
1371. But they must be t___d and applied. Try to form them into h___ts!		tried habits
1372. Make it a h___ to control your unreasonable and irrational worries and fears.		habit

1373. If you fear one particular action or thing, it is best to __ __ .
    a) forget it
    b) love it
    c) hate it
    d) do it
		d) do it

1374. Make it a habit to bring the things you fear out into the open and f___ up to them squarely.		face
1375. After you've done all you can to p____e for or eliminate major fears, accept the in_____.		prepare inevitable
1376. Minimize the effects on you as best you can and then _____ the inevitable.		accept
1377. Stop being afraid of the future. Take care of the p_____ and the future will take care of itself.		present

1378. _____ ___ the things you fear whenever you can.
    a) Prepare for
    b) Beware of
    c) Look for
    d) Forget about
		a) Prepare for

1379. Talk about your fears. Don't b___ them up inside you.		bottle
1380. Set aside ___ special day to think of all your fears.		one
1381. Again, I must be repetitive, and remind you that these rules, ideas and suggestions must be used in order for them to work or be of any help to you. ___ the suggestions! COURSE #5 BEGINS ON THE NEXT SHEET.		Use

COURSE #5: HOW TO MAKE PEOPLE DO WHAT YOU WANT

1382. Another very important part of mind power and mind organization is learning how to deal with, and handle, people both in business and social life. Dealing with p____ is an art.		people
1383. The most useful asset in business and in life itself, is knowing how to d__l with, and handle, people.		deal
1384. You can acquire this art by doing two things. First, by learning to understand the underlying principles behind it; and second, by practicing these pr____s in all dealings and relations with people.		principles
1385. This entire section will be used to teach you how to do these things. The rules and suggestions are all applicable to either social or business dealings. Use the suggestions to better your business and executive ability and also to better your personal and s___l relations.		social
1386. It is first necessary for you to realize that the craving for appreciation is the deepest feeling of human nature. Everyone wants to be app_____d, to be thought of as a unique <u>individual</u>.		appreciated
1387. It boils down to the law of <u>self-interest</u>. Self-interest; the craving for app_____n, is the core of human nature.		appreciation
1388. Every person is the center and hub of his own little universe. Each one of us is interested in, and concerned with, himself first and foremost. We are the c___r or hub of our own world.		center
1389. Everything that ever happens within our ken, or sphere, is thought of in terms of how does it affect <u>me</u>. All that's basically important to most of us is, <u>my</u> hunger, <u>my</u> pain, <u>my</u> house, ___ interests, etc.		my
1390. It has been found that we all use the words, I, me, mine, etc., more than any others. As a matter of fact, about every <u>fifth</u> word we use is a derivative of the word, ___.		my

1391. Self-in____; the center-of-his-own-world feeling is the motivating force of life.		interest
1392. Anything anyone ever does, particularly when told to, is because it serves their self-_____.		interest
1393. If you can get to understand and use these principles, you have at your command the most powerful tool for d____g with people.		dealing
1394. Each person is the c____r of his own world of experience and action. Each p____n basically understands only his own world.		center person
1395. In order for any individual to appreciate anything it must serve his self-_____; must satisfy his craving for app____tion.		interest appreciation
1396. To deal with p____ effectively, each person must be so handled, regarded and treated.		people
1397. The wish for worth; the desire to be important, is the deepest urge in human nature. It is man's deepest wish to be im_____.		important
1398. You must learn to deal with each person so as to cause him to feel that he's the center; that he's unique and imp____.		important
1399. Always remember that getting a man to think well of you is nowhere as essential as getting him to th___ well of himself!		think

1400. This, of course, may go against your nature at first, but you must learn to do it. Form the h__t of getting people to th___ well of themselves.		habit think
1401. Deal with people as if they exist. Always know and use a person's name. If you've studied my section on remembering names and faces, you'll have no trouble r_____ing their n___s.		remembering names
1402. Just as each man is the center of his own world, his n___ is his most prized possession. Always use it appropriately and respectfully.		name
1403. Try to remember not only his name and face, but any facts you can about him. This shows that you regard each p____n as an im_____t individual.		person important
1404. Justice Felix Frankfurter said that "Courtesy is the lubricant of society." It is. Each time you're c_____s to a person, you're showing interest, recognition and awareness of that person.		courteous
1405. Use the two most beautiful words, "Thank you," more often and you'll hear them more o__n.		often
1406. There is always time for c_____y. Stop using excuses for avoiding it. Keep in mind that other people have troubles, pains, are busy, etc. - just as you do.		courtesy
1407. Learn to show people genuine interest, understanding, respect and c_____y and you'll be able to get them to do the things you want them to do.		courtesy
1408. The best way to make people like you and make them do what you w___ them to is to be interested in other people's interests! There's no better way of gaining their attention and respect.		want

1409. You may have to feign this interest at first. Just <u>act in</u>_____d, and soon you'll find you won't have to act.		interested
1410. Start practicing to listen; I mean really <u>listen</u>. It is almost impossible to separate attentive listening and in____t.		interest
1411. They go together. In order to l___ well, get interested. If you find it difficult to get interested, start listening attentively. One helps accomplish the other.		listen
1412. Stop talking so much about your favorite subject, <u>you</u>. Talk about the other person <u>to</u> that person. Show in_____t in the projects, troubles, ambitions and general interests of the other person.		interest
1413. If you want to develop executive ability, or learn to handle people in general, make it your business to find out the special in_____s of the person.		interests
1414. Everyone is as egocentric as you are. Get people to talk about themselves; what they've done, what they'd like to do, what they're in_____ed in or proud of.		interested
1415. Most people are vain, and if you follow the above suggestions, you will flatter their vanities. Self-preservation and self-_____ is the core of man.		interest
1416. Control these forces with skill and tact and you multiply their power. Successful leaders and executives have learned to harness these f___s in their dealings with people.		forces
1417. To summarize: Remember that every man is the c___r of his own world. He wants to feel im_____t, be well-known, have worth.		center important

1418. Always deal with him, therefore, as an im_____ individual. Make him think well of himself .		important
1419. Know and use his n____. Show attention, respect, in____t and c_____y. Allow him to talk about his own interests and accomplishments.		name interest courtesy
1420. In other words, allow the person to be proud and to express that p___ .		pride
1421. The self-in_____ , center-of-the-world feeling in all men is a powerful driving force. Learn to put it to work for you! Recognize it in others and they will do anything in the world for you.		interest
1422. Another rule is to show confidence in people, both in business and socially. It is important to show c_____ce in other people's ability and integrity.		confidence
1423. You have to train yourself to believe that most people are capable of doing just a little better than they themselves think they can. Do that, and you'll inspire c_____ce.		confidence
1424. Show that you trust people, and you'll usually bring out the best in them. As an executive, it's a good idea to delegate jobs and then stop worrying about them. Expect good results and more often than not, you'll get good r____s.		results
1425. Just go a bit out of your way to t___t people and you'll find that they're usually trustworthy. You've seen the 'honor system' newsstands all over the country; people are put on their honor and the stands haven't lost any money yet.		trust
1426. The best way of building (or re-building) responsibility and self-reliance is to show c_____ce in those who need the building or rebuilding.		confidence

164

1427. Warden Lewis E. Lawes of Sing Sing always maintained that if a criminal in his prison was treated as an honorable man, he was flattered and responded because he was proud that someone t____ed him.		trusted
1428. To show c_____ce in others, ask for their help or advice whenever you can. Most people will like you and respond to you if you ask them for help and ad____.		confidence advice
1429. It's quite easy to advise others and difficult not to. Remember that if friends ask for your _____ they usually want you to tell them exactly what they've already made up their minds to do.		advice
1430. If you feel you must give a_____ , tell people to do what you think or feel they want to do.		advice
1431. You instill liking and c_____ce when you occasionally ask others for advice or help. It makes them feel that you have confidence in them. You're feeding their egos and they'll like you better for it.		confidence
1432. Another idea on how to show confidence is to indicate your high expectations of people by assigning and awarding title and/or position. Such c_____ce, well placed, usually elicits the expected response.		confidence
1433. Learn to expect others to be pleasant and chances are they will be. People are likely to be, or do, or come up to what you e____t of them.		expect
1434. If you really do this, you'll find yourself acting accordingly. Most people will act toward you as you ___ toward them. Use the rule of 'similar attitudes.		act
1435. Try smiling (or frowning) at the next person you talk to. The odds are he'll s___ (or frown) right back at you. Act as if you're looking in a mirror when talking to others.		smile

1436. The image you send into it will come out of it. People's attitudes and actions are usually reflections of your own attitudes and a_____s.		actions
1437. In most instances, you stand a much better chance of getting the results you want if you <u>expect</u> them, and more important, let it be <u>known</u> that you _____ them.		expect
1438. It is a fact that with a little encouragement (and latitude) people, by nature, like to prove themselves better than they are, or b___r than others think they are.		better
1439. So, to show c_____ce in others, – and to get them to do what you want them to do – indicate that you believe the person can do better than he himself thinks he can.		confidence
1440. Occasionally, ask for help and a ____. Even ask a favor of the person.		advice
1441. Let the person know that you have high _____ s of his ability. a) hopes b) feelings c) ways d) expectations		d) expectations
1442. Utilizing these rules and suggestions properly will make people like you and help you to make them do what you want them to do. You realize that there is only <u>one</u> way to make people do what you____ them to.		want
1443. That one way is to make <u>him</u> want to do it. Now then, <u>how</u> can you get a man to <u>want</u> to do what <u>you</u> desire? First and foremost, find out what <u>he</u> really w___s!		wants
1444. High pressure selling, forcing, bullying, etc., won't do it. Making people want (or <u>think</u> they want) what you w___ , is the only way.		want

1445. Many important negotiations and successful businesses have been founded on just this principle. Good insurance salesmen find out what prospective clients w___ , then sell them insurance.		want
1446. Each man has his n___s and desires. Find out what they are! Big or small, the need and worry is basically the same.		needs
1447. Whether a man wants to secure his (and his family's) next meal, or insure his son's education, or his daughter's wedding; or, if a man is thinking of how to secure another company to add to his corporation, the n__d is the same.		need
1448. Find out what a person's needs, desires and wants are. Then use those w___s to get him to do what you want.		wants
1449. Demonstrate how it will benefit a man to do what you want! Say you want a position with a particular firm. During your interview try stressing what you can do, or how you can serve the firm, instead of how securing the position is what you w__.		want
1450. It is important to find out what people really want, make them see it and then show how you can help them get it. And at the same time, getting them to do what you w___.		want
1451. Don't think of only material things. Feeding, or enlarging, a man's ego, making him feel important, is just as powerful a tool. You've got to show how doing what you want will make him feel im_____.		important
1452. Remember, show that it will give him power and im_____ce to do what you want him to do.		importance
1453. Feed his ego. Telling a man that you can't see why with his personality, etc., he doesn't do such and such – is halfway to getting him to d_ it.		do

1454. You can make people do what you w___ them to, by making them feel superior! "I would do this if I had your knowledge, your personality, your sense of humor, etc., etc."		want
1455. Let people know you're depending on them because of their su____r ability, knowledge, personality.		superior
1456. Make it obvious that you have t__t in someone's advice, judgment and ability and it will be easier to get him to do anything you w___ him to.		trust want
1457. Then show how doing this thing will bring him prestige and approval of others! Or, that failure to do what you want will bring loss of p____ge.		prestige
1458. And always try to make it easy and attractive and interesting for him to do the thing you ____ him to do.		want
1459. So to summarize: In order to get people to do what you want, you have to make them w___ it first.		want
1460. Make it your business to find out what he really w___s. Then demonstrate that what you w___ will benefit him, and get what he wants.		wants want
1461. Show that it will bring him power, prestige and approval of others if he does the thing you want. Work on the big three: money, power and p____ge.		prestige
1462. Always make it easy, attractive and int____ing for him to do it. Start applying and practicing these principles now, and it will become easy for you to make people like you and do the things you w___ them to.		interesting want

1463. Now, when he does something for you, learn how to show appreciation. This is one of the biggest assets in dealing with people. Show app____n.		appreciation
1464. The old saying, "You can catch more flies with honey than with vinegar," holds true when dealing with p____.		people
1465. Experiments prove that people receiving praise or app____n improve most in their work; people getting reproof rate next, and those receiving neither show the least improvement.		appreciation
1466. I've already told you that the desire to be appreciated is the deepest feeling or desire of human nature, so make a habit of showing app____n.		appreciation
1467. Let me go over one or two rules on how to show appreciation. First, remember the little things. As I've already mentioned, remember to use those two words, "Thank you." Show courtesy. Remember n__s, and facts about others.		names
1468. Remember the little t____s. Practice making a h____t of showing a____n. It's easy to acquire the habit and it brings wonderful results and profits!		things habit appreciation
1469. Nowadays, unfortunately, most deeds of thoughtfulness, kindness, etc., are taken for granted. Why don't you be different; don't take them for g____d; show appreciation.		granted
1470. Show particular appreciation for outstanding achievements. This a____n is sometimes more important than financial reward.		appreciation
1471. Failure to give credit destroys morale. So remember to always give c__t and show apprecia- tion to employees and friends.		credit

1472. Successful leaders of men have the capacity to take a deep interest in other people's problems and to show sympathetic understanding. Get in_____d in other people's problems _if_ you want them to do what you want.		interested
1473. Learn to compliment people sincerely and appropriately. Find out the special abilities of people and c_____t them on that ability.		compliment
1474. C_____t people on what they're proud of.		compliment
1475. So, practice acquiring the habit of showing a_____n.		appreciation
1476. At the same time, learn how to save a man's face if he's made a mistake. Most people are usually already upset over their m____e; don't add insult to injury.		mistake
1477. It will not help you either to have people like you or to get them to do what you want if you mortify a person who has made a mistake. Rather, try to help him save ___.		face
1478. Some rules on how to help a man ____ face. Talk to him about it _alone_. Do not criticize in the presence of o___s.		save others
1479. Even if criticism is necessary, preface it with a compliment. "You've been doing better at this job than anyone we've had, but we have to straighten out this particular, etc. etc." Cr____e if you must, but try to com_____t at the same time.		criticize compliment
1480. A good way to deal with disciplinary situations is to ask a man how he would discipline _himself_. He knows he must be disciplined, but ask _his_ suggestions on the extent of the d_____e.		discipline

1481. Ask a man how he would correct his <u>own</u> mistakes and you'll feed his ego. And, he'll usually set up more stringent d____e for himself than you would, and he can't dislike you for it.		discipline
1482. Try to get the person to <u>participate</u> in the common problem. <u>Make</u> it a common problem; you're <u>all</u> interested in solving it. Remember, if the problem does not touch his self-in____ , he doesn't really care.		interest
1483. Get the person to p____ate in the problem, and its solution.		participate
1484. Finally, if there is no remedy, if you must fire a man, attempt to help him find another job. Fire him if you must, but do attempt to h__ him at the same time.		help
1485. Above all, and what all this is teaching you, consider the other guy's pride! The more delicate a situation, the more important it is to help him save f__ .		face

1486. To help a man save face, talk to him about his mistake
    a) after hours
    b) alone
    c) loudly
    d) in the presence of others
		b) alone

1487. If you must criticize, try to _____ at the same time.
    a) cry
    b) shout
    c) laugh
    d) compliment
		d) compliment

1488. If you must use disciplinary action, ask a man how he would d_____e himself.		discipline

1489. Try to get a person to _____ in the common problem.
    a) participate
    b) wallow
    c) forget
    d) remember
		a) participate

1490. Above all, consider the other guy's ____ and help him save face.
    a) wife
    b) money
    c) pride
    d) mistake
		c) pride

1491. The following frames have some good suggestions and rules on how to handle p_____ generally, in business and socially.		people
1492. In business dealings particularly and all dealings with people, in general - try making a request instead of giving a com____ or order. Don't treat employees as if they were machines.		command
1493. Make all decisions with regard to others. Listen to grievances. Remember that your decisions may effect others; make them with r____d to others.		regard
1494. Accept and use suggested ideas whenever possible; and make it a h___t to personally recognize ability.		habit
1495. Try to follow the established lines of authority in business. Don't go over other people's heads. Basically, I'm telling you to always see and understand the other p____n's point of view.		person's
1496. Failure to see the other guy's point of ____, blacks out everyone but yourself and causes trouble in all human relations.		view
1497. The ability to put yourself in his place and see his ____ of view, is the core of learning how to deal with people.		point
1498. It will help you to see the other person's ____ of ____ if you follow these suggestions. First; listen to him.		point view

172

1499. Make an effort to <u>understand</u> the other p___n.		person
1500. Always ask yourself how your actions and attitudes affect the other person. If you're not sure, ask someone who might anticipate the effects better than you. Think of the effects of your a_____ns on the other person.		actions
1501. It's important to ask someone else if you have to, because your sense of fairness and judgment may be much different from those with whom you're dealing. Ask _____ else if you're not sure.		someone
1502. Ask <u>yourself</u> if you'd be willing to do or accept what <u>you're asking</u> the other person to do or a___t.		accept
1503. Some more suggestions for personal contacts: Prefix requests or orders with softening statements such as, "I'd appreciate it if ..." or, "How do <u>you</u> think it should be done," etc. Use a s_____ing statement whenever you can.		softening
1504. "I believe; it's my opinion; don't you agree," and so on, can s___n definite statements. This can save you much f____ later on.		soften face
1505. An important tip: Remember that most people have a tendency to imitate! Behavior in <u>yourself</u> will induce corresponding or similar b_____r in others.		behavior
1506. <u>Do</u> as you want others to do, and they'll tend to do <u>it</u>. You cannot expect loyalty from friends and employees if you are not l___ yourself.		loyal
1507. To conclude this section:- There are two main ways of <u>inducing</u> desired actions in others. One, by <u>doing</u> what you w___ others to do, and two, by <u>suggestion</u>.		want

1508.　The best way to guide someone's action is to g___ his thinking.		guide
1509.　Try not to merely issue orders and commands, guide his th___ing instead.		thinking
1510.　How do you guide a man's thinking? Guide his wanting! Guide his w___ing by showing how he can get what he wants!		wanting
1511.　So, to persuade a man to do what you want him to:- Carefully outline exactly what it is he w___s.		wants
1512.　Show him how your plan of actions can get it for him; and finally give him concrete evidence that your plan of a___ns will work.		actions
1513.　If he doesn't agree at first, don't contradict or argue. Ask questions which will expose weaknesses or consequences he may not have foreseen. Don't contradict or ____, ask questions to bring out your point instead.		argue
1514.　Introduce qualifications that may alter his opinion. Try to make it easy for him to abandon his former negative position. Make sure you set it up so that he doesn't lose f___ by doing so.		face
1515.　It's wise to plan strategy in trying to guide people. Know exactly what you're going to say, and try to anticipate reactions to what you say. Know not only your position, but how to sell that pos____n.		position
1516.　Don't try to convince a man against his will. "A man convinced against his ____ is of the same opinion still."		will

1517. No; better to sell him on your idea. Get him as enthusiastic about it as you are. People respond in kind. If you're enthusiastic, he'll be en_____c.		enthusiastic
1518. Give him some motivation; get the idea working in his mind. Get his self-in_____ working for you.		interest
1519. In other words, if you can get your goal operating in him, he'll do what you w___ him to, because it's what he wants, too!		want
1520. Okay; get your g__l operating in the other fellow by:- Stating the goal. Make sure he understands exactly what the g__l is.		goal goal
1521. State the goal so that he definitely un_____s it, then make sure he knows what benefits it will produce for him; for his future; for h__ prestige; for h__ self-interest.		understands his his
1522. Listen to his ideas and incorporate them whenever possible. L_____ to his objections and soothe them whenever possible.		Listen
1523. Be sure to always check his efforts, performance and progress. He must know that his work and e_____ts will be evaluated and appreciated.		efforts
1524. Another rule is:- Get your g__l operating in the other person by rewarding. By r_____ing both materially and psychologically.		goal rewarding
1525. And finally, by reminding him over and over again, of that goal. R_____d him of the _____ and how it benefits him.		Remind goal

1526. If you can get your ___ operating in the other fellow, you'll be guiding his thinking, and he'll do what you want.		goal
1527. He'll do what you want because it's what he ___ s, too.		wants
1528. State the goal so that he un_____ds it. Make sure he sees how it will benefit him. Get his self-in_____ working for you.		understands interest
1529. Incorporate h_s ideas when you can. Listen to and soothe h_ objections. Always check his efforts; and r___d him both materially and psychologically.		his his reward
1530. Remind him of the ___ and its benefits to him over and over again.		goal
1531. Well, by now I'm sure you understand the underlying principles of how to deal with and handle people. It all boils down to the principle of self-_____ and the center-of-the-world feeling which is deeply imbedded in all people.		interest
1532. Work with these principles, never against them. Apply all the rules, ideas and suggestions I've given you, consistently, and they will become h__t.		habit
1533. Make them a habit and you'll never again have any trouble at all in handling, and d__ing with p____.		dealing people
YOU HAVE NOW COMPLETED COURSE #5 OF HARRY LORAYNE'S <u>INSTANT MIND POWER</u> TEACHING-MACHINE. COURSE #6 BEGINS ON THE NEXT SHEET.	No answer required.	

176

COURSE #6: HOW TO CREATE WINNING IDEAS

1534. Every new business started with an <u>idea</u>. Every new product started with an idea. Every new way of advertising, or selling, or packaging, etc., started with an i___.		idea
1535. Ideas, imagination, creative thinking – these are the surest formulas for success. Learn to think creatively and you're on your way to s____s.		success
1536. Most of our big companies pay big money for ideas that will save <u>them</u> m____ or produce more business. Employee suggestion plans are now being used in many big businesses.		money
1537. Most everyone has heard the story of the man who made a fortune by telling the Coca Cola Company to "bottle it." General Motors alone has rewarded new i___s with over ten million dollars.		ideas
1538. Business always changes; it <u>will</u> always ch___e. So there is always room and need for new i___s.		change ideas
1539. The people who come up with the ideas that help business to ch___e will find their bank accounts changing and <u>growing</u> even faster.		change
1540. How can <u>you</u> think creatively and come up with new i___s? Well, anyone can, but it takes practice just like anything else!		ideas
1541. That's right. If you <u>practice</u> kindness, you'll become kinder; if you <u>practice</u> courage, you'll become more courageous; if you pr____e thinking creatively, you'll come up with new ideas.		practice
1542. Unfortunately, most of us today have fallen into mental ruts that are difficult to climb out of. Years ago, when people <u>had</u> to think creatively in order to live, c____e thinking came a bit easier.		creative

177

1543. Nowadays, I think most of us would rather exert ourselves physically than mentally. Sure; it's easier to do physical work than to think. Well, not if you p____e creative thinking.		practice
1544. Many people feel that the ability to think creatively is something you have to be born with. Well, they're right; you do! And most of us <u>are</u> born with the ability to ____ creatively.		think
1545. No; imagination is <u>not</u> a special gift. <u>You</u> can think c____ly if you want to work at it. <u>It's</u> really nothing more than an <u>habitual</u> way of thinking in a certain way. Let me show you how:		creatively
1546. There are definite <u>rules</u> you must follow to practice thinking creatively, and they are rules you've already been using all along. Either consciously or subconsciously, you've already used the r___s that help you produce new ideas.		rules
1547. I'm just going to pinpoint these rules and techniques for you. Follow them consciously and conscientiously and you're on your way to developing your cr____ve ability.		creative
1548. All right. Let's start. Anything and everything can be done differently. There is <u>nothing</u> that can't be changed. No matter how <u>it's being</u> done now, it isn't necessarily being done the <u>best</u> way. Anything can be ch___d.		changed
1549. Things can be packaged differently; things can be made differently; things can be sold differently; things can be <u>done</u> d_____y; and so on, ad infinitum.		differently
1550. Why would, or should, anything be done d_____y? To get it done better and more efficiently.		differently
1551. This brings us to the first rule for strengthening your creative powers. <u>Locate Or Zero In On A Need!</u> Pick out <u>anything</u>; any product, service or procedure, think about it, and locate or zero in on a ____.		need

1552. What about the product should be changed for the better? There is always something. Many things if you look at it long enough. Z___ in on a need.		Zero
1553. Ask yourself questions like, "Would this be better or more practical if it were larger? Smaller? Rounder? Heavier? Lighter? and so forth. Ask these q_____s and try to answer them.		questions
1554. Ask yourself "Is this too small? Should it be made l___r?"		larger
1555. Or ask, "Is this too large? Can it be made s____r?"		smaller
1556. Or ask, "Is it too light? Can it be made h____r?"		heavier
1557. Or ask, "Is it too heavy? Can it be made l____r?" And so on. There are dozens of q_____s you can ask about anything.		lighter questions
1558. Asking yourself a q_____n about anything and trying to find an answer will start your imagination working. It will help you l____ a need.		question locate
1559. Did anything annoy you today? Did you come up against any particular problem? Good! Each time you recognize a problem, you've taken your first step toward creating an i__.		idea
1560. Select any procedure at your office; go over it in your mind step by step. Try to find something wrong or inefficient about it. Ask yourself q_____s about each st__.		questions step

1561. Remember, each time you find a problem or something wrong, you're on your way to c____g an idea.		creating
1562. Finding the problem, l____ing a need, is the nucleus of creative thinking!		locating
1563. Try it now. Select anything (product or service) and try to locate a n__d. Find a way it can be done better. Anything can be done b___r.		need better
1564. You know that the auto manufacturers try to come up with something new every year. Even if a product doesn't need something n__, that something new can sell more of it.		new
1565. Telephones didn't need colors, or different models, but those ideas have brought the phone companies much more business. So think of any product or service and find or create a n__ or a way of selling more of it.		need
1566. Ask yourself one question at a time; then work on that question. If you can't get anywhere with that, ask another q_____, and so on.		question
1567. Remember, you can't have ideas without n___s. Find a true problem and you've found a real need. You've started to think cr_____ly.		needs creatively
1568. Now, let's assume you've found the need. The next step is to ask yourself WHY does this need or problem exist. Perhaps there's a good reason. Find out w__. Think about w__. Ask yourself __?		why why why
1569. If you come up with an answer, "Because it's cheaper to make it that way," or "Because the consumer likes it that way" - challenge that reason. Ask yourself why; then ch_____e the answer you come up with.		challenge

180

1570. Your reason may be valid. Then again, it may not. If it is v___d, go on to another problem, another need.		valid
1571. If you feel it isn't valid, keep worrying it. Here's a need that needs fulfilling; there's no valid reason why it hasn't been fulfilled. Ask w__ again! W__ hasn't it been fulfilled?		why Why
1572. Do you understand? Keep asking w__ and keep challenging your own answers and reasons. Sooner or later you'll come to the end of the question and answer road. And – all along that road – you've been thinking cr_____y.		why creatively
1573. As a matter of fact, an i___ may have already formed in your mind from these q_____s.		idea questions
1574. So – the first rule to help you think creatively is to l___e or zero in on a ___.		locate need
1575. Even if a need doesn't exist, it can be created. Locate or create a ___.		need
1576. To help you do this, find a pr___m. Once you've done this, ask yourself, why. Ask yourself ___ and keep challenging your answers and reasons.		problem why
1577. When you've finally reached the end of the question-and-answer road, proceed to the next rule:- Find The Simple Solution! You've already started to strengthen your creative powers; continue, and find the s_____ to the need or problem you've located or created.		solution
1578. In most cases, the s_____ will be a simple one. It might even be an obvious one. Obvious after it's found; perhaps so o____s that nobody thought of it before.		solution obvious

1579. Please keep in mind that in applying these rules, you are prone to i___s. You're making yourself available to them.		ideas
1580. After a while i___s will come to you from all directions and from almost anything you see or hear. For now, I'm afraid you'll have to hunt for them; work at it. Follow these rules.		ideas
1581. To help you find the solution: Most new ideas are simply a combination of things you already know! Try applying s____ns that already exist (answers to other problems) to your current p____m.		solutions problem
1582. Take s____ns from other areas. Combine them and you may come up with a new solution sooner than you think. C____e two or more solutions from other fields. Try to find the n__ solution anywhere you can.		solutions combine new
1583. Practice going outside of the field in which your particular interest lies. If the problem you're working on is in the selling field, it isn't necessary to look only in that field. Practice looking o____ of your field.		outside
1584. Sometimes a complete solution can be taken from one field and brought intact to yours. This will be a new i___ in your field because no one did it or thought of it before.		idea
1585. The idea for power steering for cars came from trucks. And, it was originally used in ships! So think outside your own f___d.		field
1586. Perhaps I can illustrate in this way. Here is the Roman Numeral IX. Can you add one symbol to this and ch____ the 9 to a 6? IX		change
1587. Well, have you come up with an answer? If not, you're restricting your thinking to only Roman Numerals. Don't restrict your th___ing. Look outside of Roman Numerals. IX		thinking

182

1588. If you haven't reached the solution yet – simply put an 's' in front of the IX; that makes the IX a $\overline{\text{SIX}}$ (6). See? Don't r____ct your thinking.		restrict

1589. Look at these nine dots in a square:
  .   .   .
  .   .   .
  .   .   .
(see next frame)		

1589. The pr____m is to draw four straight lines, all connected, $\overline{\text{that}}$ go through or touch, <u>all</u> the dots. You must do it without removing the pencil from the paper and without crossing a line twice.
  .   .   .
  .   .   .
  .   .   .
		problem

1590. .   .   .   Have you found the simple
  .   .   .   solution? If not, stop re-
  .   .   .   ____ing your thinking. No
one told you that the four lines had to stay <u>within</u> the square! Before you move to the next frame, try it again.
		restricting

1591. Do you see how this was solved by moving o____e the area of the square and also o____e the area in which you were think- ing? Don't place re_____ns on your thinking .		outside outside restrictions
1592. Practice thinking from all viewpoints; try all possibilities. Do this, and you're adding more power to your c____ve thinking ability.		creative
1593. I could go on giving you example after example, but I don't think it's necessary. You simply have to practice looking <u>anywhere</u> for the simple s__tions.		solutions
1594. And, you have countless places to look! Anything you've ever done, anything you've ever experienced – has given you a backlog of ideas and s____ns just waiting to be used.		solutions
1595. Draw from any and a__ of your experiences to find that s____n.		all solution

1596. Combine ideas. Try anything in combination with your p____m or need; see if it fits. Twist it, turn it, examine it every which way.		problem
1597. After all, the steam engine is really not much more than an exaggeration of the idea of the tea kettle! A doctor came up with the i___ of the stethoscope when he recalled how a hollow log carried sound.		idea
1598. All right. The first rule for strengthening your creative ability is:- L____ and zero in on a ____.		Locate need
1599. After you've found that need (or problem), go to the next rule:- Find the simple s_____n.		solution
1600. To get this solution, try to go outside your own f____.		field
1601. Just reading, or knowing, these two rules won't help you much. You've got to actually get into the habit of applying them. I suggest you get some paper and try them now! Try the r___s.		rules
1602. First apply all the sub-rules and hints I gave you for locating a n___. Locate it and then keep asking w__. Keep asking why; ch_____ all your answers, until you've reached bedrock. You can go no further.		need why challenge
1603. Now you come to the more important step; find the simple s_____n. Write a list of solutions. Work for quantity here; list at least twenty; then l__t some more!		solution list
1604. What you're doing now is what successful idea men and creative people always do; you're 'brainstorming.' L__t any and all possible s_____ns, no matter how silly, ridiculous, crazy or impractical.		List solutions

184

1605. That is exactly what br_____ing is! Get it out! Get it on paper! That's more than half your battle. Sometimes the silliest or most ridiculous possibility will be the final answer!		brainstorming
1606. Even if it isn't, the final simple solution may come <u>from</u> one of your silly ideas. Make it a <u>challenge</u> and a game! Ch_____ yourself to <u>list more</u> wild or silly s_____ns.		Challenge solutions
1607. Try it. List anything that comes to mind. At first you may be able to l__t only one or two s_____ns, but then they'll <u>start</u> coming to you. The only way you can prove this is by <u>trying</u> it.		list solutions
1608. Right now, <u>at this moment</u>, you alone have the choice of acquiring the ability of cr_____ imagination or not! Don't think you'll try this brainstorming later; try it <u>now</u>! If you don't at least t__ now, you probably never will!		creative try
1609. And don't stop listing the s_____. Remember, <u>the</u> right one may come to you within the next three or four you put down on paper.		solutions
1610. Dr. Ehrlich's great medical contribution to humanity was called "666", because it was the 666th s_____n he had tried! And, he would have <u>tried 666 more</u> if he hadn't found it when he did!		solution

1611. Okay; you can think creatively if you follow these rules:- First, select <u>any</u> product or service, in your business or not, and _____ or zero in on a need.
    a) cause
    b) think about
                (see next frame)
	Your answer should go below ↓	

1611. (continued)
 	
    c) confide in
    d) locate
		d) locate

1612. Find what you can about the product or service which can, or should be, changed for the
 	
_____.
    a) money
    b) better
    c) worst
    d) fun of it
		b) better

185

1613. Each time you recognize a _____ , you've taken your first step toward thinking creatively.
  a) problem
  b) friend
  c) product
  d) price
		a) problem

1614. If and when you've located a need, ask yourself ___ it exists.
  a) if
  b) who
  c) why
  d) when
		c) why

1615. Then keep _____ your answers and reasons.
  a) writing
  b) reading
  c) believing
  d) challenging
		d) challenging

1616. When you've really pinpointed a need, start trying to find the simple _____ .
  a) solution
  b) way out
  c) problem
  d) cause
		a) solution

1617. Most often the solution will be a _____ of things or answers you already know.
  a) group
  b) combination
  c) answer
  d) surplus
		b) combination

1618. Try going o___ e your own field for solutions.		outside

1619. Try all areas, possibilities and viewpoints. Don't _____ your thinking.
  a) crowd
  b) believe
  c) restrict
  d) cloud
		c) restrict

1620. When you list all the solutions that come to you, no matter how half-formed, improbable or crazy, you're doing what all successful idea men do. You're _____ .
  a) procrastinating
  b) ridiculing
  (see next frame)
	Your answer should go below ♦	

1620. (continued)
 	
  c) associating
  d) brainstorming
		d) brainstorming

186

1621. You'll be pleased with the next rule, because you don't have to do anything. It is:- <u>Let Your Subconscious Go To Work</u>! Which means you don't have to do a ____ g.		anything
1622. I'm sure that, many times, you've had good ideas just come to you. <u>But</u> - did they <u>really</u> just pop out of nowhere? Think about it; wasn't it an answer to a p____ m you'd been consciously struggling with in the past?		problem
1623. The point is, 'inspiration' will usually come to you <u>because</u> you spent some time wrestling with the problem in the p__t.		past
1624. So; after following my first two rules to locate and solve any p____ m, and after trying your darndest and going as far as you <u>can</u> with the s____ n, just forget it for the time being!		problem solution
1625. You don't have to do a thing; just f__ t it. But you see, your subconscious is going to keep right on working on the problem anyway!		forget
1626. When you apply the first two rules you've gone from 'low gear' into 'high gear.' Now, forget it and let your sub____ s mind go into 'idle.' Don't do a thing; you have no control over your subconscious anyway.		subconscious
1627. Of course, the fact that you <u>have</u> applied the first two rules, is what puts your s____ s to work on the problem. You cannot receive the bonus of this third rule if you don't apply the first two.		subconscious
1628. It may take hours, days or minutes, but solutions <u>will</u> come to you! Again, you need only try it to prove it. Let your s____ s go to work.		subconscious
1629. Now then, the more p____ ms you're working on, the more your subconscious has to work on, the more ideas or answers it may come up with.		problems

1630. So it's wise to try to apply these rules to many things at a time. Your subconscious is going to work anyway, you may as well have it work on the things you want it to. Feed it gas, let it idle, and watch the i___s come!		ideas
1631. Remember this: The greater your creative activity, the greater will become your ____ve ability!		creative
1632. Believe me, 'inspiration' will come. Sir Isaac Newton saw an apple fall and the world romanticized that the complete law of gravity came to him at that moment. Nothing could be farther from the truth. He'd been working on, and thinking of, the p____m for some time.		problem
1633. I mention this to point out that accidents and odd happenings can be opportunities. They can remind you of something or be the thing you're looking for to combine or correlate in order to find your s_____n.		solution
1634. The chance occurrence is not important; you are. You can get ideas; occurrences can't. But the chance o____nce may be just the element you're looking for; or, it may trigger your sub-conscious.		occurrence
1635. Give your curiosity free rein. Capitalize on anything that you see, or that happens, which stirs your imagination. Ask yourself q____ns about it.		questions
1636. Rudyard Kipling wrote about his six honest serving men; Where, What, When, Why, How, and Who. Put some of them to w__k for you!		work
1637. When you see or experience anything, ask yourself, "How can I utilize this; where or when or how, can I u____e it?"		utilize
1638. Basically, if you make it a habit to a_ about anything, "How can I use this; how can it be of value to me?" your creative p___rs will be strengthened each time; and, you'll be finding those solutions more often!		ask powers

1639. So remember, after you've gone as far as possible applying the first two rules, and you haven't come up with an idea yet, let your sub-_____ go to work!		subconscious
1640. Try to make it a habit to carry a notebook and pencil with you always. Don't let those precious thoughts or ideas escape. When your subconscious lets an i___ get into your conscious mind, you want to get it down on paper immediately.		idea
1641. Here's an idea I call 'memory nudgers.' You're in bed, about to fall asleep, and a good idea comes to you. How're you going to re_____r it when you get up in the morning?		remember
1642. Well, just reach over to your night-table and lay your clock face down, or turn it away from you. Or, put your ashtray on the floor; or dump some cigarettes out of the pack onto the table or floor. Do anything within reach that you'll be sure to notice in the m_____g!		morning
1643. When you notice the thing that's out of place or order, in the morning, it will remind you that an i___ came to you in the middle of the night!		idea
1644. Of course, there may still be the problem of r_____ing what the idea was! So, perhaps, the best thing is to have your notebook and pencil on your night-table. But you might try the 'memory nudger' idea and see if it works for you.		remembering
1645. All right. If too much time elapses without reaching that s_____n, go back to your original notes, go over those ideas again.		solution
1646. Some of the i___s you listed may seem close to the solution, but just not right yet. Work on those. Pick one and change it a little here and a little there. Twist and manipulate it. Do the same with the next one.		ideas
1647. Sooner or later, the complete s_____n or idea will come to you. It has to; everything's work- ing for you. And don't let the word, 'work' scare you. "Inspiration is 90% perspiration!"		solution

1648. The other 10% is the know-how! You're getting _that_ here and now. Just be sure you try and apply them. You're on your way to being able to think c_____ly.		creatively
1649. Another important tip: - Make it a h___t to _finish_ any creative effort you start!		habit
1650. Even if you feel it will be unsuccessful, bring it to some sort of culmination. If you have a plan for a new procedure for your office, f_____ it, get it down on paper even if you think you'll tear it up when you're through.		finish
1651. If you start to write a story, f_____ it. Aside from the fact that I want you to get into the h___t of finishing anything you start, many times something you've created that seems worthless to you may turn out to have merit.		finish habit
1652. And, one i___ will usually start a flow of other ideas.		idea
1653. All right; now the final rule:- Put It To The Test! Your idea has to _work_ or it's worthless. The test I'm referring to is, 'will it w__k?'		work
1654. Again, use the good old standby of asking q_____s. "Will it work? Is it practical? Is it really _better_ than what already existed?" And so on.		questions
1655. If you've come up with something _different_ but worse, obviously, you haven't been successful. It must really be b___ r		better
1656. This brings you to a very important point, _selling_ your idea. If your idea is better, ask yourself why. _Write down your answers._ You're s_ing yourself.		selling

1657. Once you've sold yourself on the idea, you're halfway to selling it to anyone else! Keep asking those questions; ___ is it better? Will it cost less? Or too much? Will it save time, money, work?		Why
1658. It may be better for you, and if this idea is for something personal, that's fine. But if it's something to be sold to your boss, or to a company, or to the public, is it b____ for them?		better
1659. Ask and answer all these questions and you're whittling the idea down to a fine point. You'll be changing, molding and maneuvering it as you go along. Most important, you're s____g yourself on the idea.		selling
1660. If your idea doesn't pass the test, don't give up! You've just located a new need (or problem)! How to make that idea pass the t___!		test
1661. So – start 'brainstorming' again! Find new ways to mold or refine. Sooner or later, it will pass the ____. Most good ideas are the result of many tries and lots of refining.		test
1662. Remember that if good i___s were easy to come by, they wouldn't be worth much! Apply the systems and techniques taught here and they'll be e__y to come by for you only.		ideas easy
1663. If you've been working along as I've been telling you to, you've most likely already produced a good ___ or two. And, you've learned a technique which will stand you in good stead for the rest of your life!		idea
1664. If you haven't produced a good idea yet, get to work. Locate or z___ in on another need and start finding the simple s____n. If you honestly and conscientiously do all this, all I've taught you, I guarantee you'll come up with good ideas!		zero solution
1665. Before leaving this section, let's summarize:– The first rule for strengthening your creative ability is, _____ or zero in on a ___.		locate need

1666. Ask yourself what about the product, service or procedure can be changed for the b____		better
1667. Try to <u>create</u> a ____ if you can't locate one.		need
1668. The second rule is:- Find the simple _____ .		solution
1669. To find that solution, c____e things and answers you already know. See if you can make them fit the problem or need.		combine
1670. Try going outside your own field. Don't r____t your thinking.		restrict
1671. Perhaps you can take an entire s____n of another problem and mold it to solve this one! Think from all viewpoints.		solution
1672. List all the wild ideas for solutions you can. Challenge yourself to list <u>more</u>. Learn to br___-____m.		brainstorm
1673. The third rule is:- Let your _____ go to work.		subconscious
1674. After applying the first two rules and getting as far as you can get for the time being, forget about it and let your subconscious go to ____ .		work

1675. Apply the rules to as many problems as possible so your _____ will have more fuel on which to idle.
    a) friends
    b) car
    c) subconscious
    d) conscious
		c) subconscious

1676. Ask questions about any unusual, or chance, occurrence. How can it be of v____ to <u>you</u>?		value
1677. If too much ti.ne passes, go back to your original notes and stir things up again. Select one idea at a time and change, twist and mold it. Give your s_____s some more fuel.		subconscious

1678. Form the habit of _____ any creative effort you start.
    a) loving
    b) finishing
    c) displaying
    d) combining
		b) finishing

1679. The final rule is:- Put it to the ____.		test
1680. Ask more q_____s. Is it really better? Is it practical? Will it cost too much? And so on.		questions
1681. Sell yourself on the idea! If it doesn't pass the test, start br_____ing again. Refine the idea or solution.		brainstorming
1682. Have you answered all the _____s in this section? Have you done the things I've told you to do? If you have, your creative ability is 100% stronger and better than it was before you picked up your pencil to answer the first question!		questions
1683. I've done all I can! It's up to you now. Go ahead and c___te ideas!		create

YOU HAVE NOW COMPLETED COURSE #6 OF HARRY LORAYNE'S <u>INSTANT MIND POWER</u> TEACHING-MACHINE. COURSE #7 BEGINS ON THE NEXT SHEET.	No answer required.	

COURSE #7: HOW TO DEVELOP STEEL-SHUTTER CONCENTRATION 1684. How would you like to be able to concentrate on anything you want to? Well, you can. Again, it's just a matter of forming a h___t.		habit
1685. Yes; like most anything else, c_____n is a habit.		concentration
1686. Also, as in anything else, it may be just a bit easier said than done. To help you, I'll give you certain definite rules to follow. Follow these rules conscientiously, and you'll acquire the habit of c_____n.		concentration
1687. In this section, I'll cover four main points. First, how to get down to work; get <u>started</u>. Then, how to concentrate on what you're reading. Third, how to c_____ on things you hear; speeches, lectures, conversations. And fourth, how to concentrate on problem-solving.		concentrate
1688. I'll discuss them one at a time. First, of course, is - getting down to work. Once you've done that, at least you've started; you're <u>trying</u> to c_____.		concentrate
1689. The worst enemy of getting started, is procrastination. I've already discussed this in the section on will power. If you've studied that section, you know that if you apply the third rule: <u>Begin</u>, and all its sub-rules, you won't be a victim of pro_____n.		procrastination
1690. All right then; just beginning is, of course, of utmost importance. But, just as important, is to <u>organize</u> the entire procedure of getting down to work. It must be attacked in an org_____d manner.		organized
1691. Organization is merely <u>planned direction</u>. It is a planned procedure, a planned system, a p_____d schedule of events or tasks.		planned
1692. To help you get down to work, which is part and parcel of concentration, you must use organization. This is simply a p_____d schedule of tasks and duties, done one after the other, in the shortest possible time and with the least amount of waste.		planned

195

1693. Organization is doing the right thing at the right time; eliminating the waste of doing the wrong thing at any time. Org_____n, for our present purposes, is basically the proper way to get down to work each day.		Organization
1694. Thinking or believing that you'll do a certain task or chore whenever you get the chance, is tantamount to neglecting it completely - you're pro_____ing.		procrastinating
1695. All right - set up a planned schedule of events for any task which requires c_____n. First and most important, set a definite time for sitting down and starting each day.		concentration
1696. Set a definite t__e each day to get started!		time
1697. Plan exactly what has to be done each day. Start at the beginning of that day's work. Do it, step by step. Plan exactly when you'll finish it, and p___ where it is you must start tomorrow!		plan
1698. Without such a definite step by step p__n of attack you must waste time generally, and in getting started particularly. Without this p____d procedure you have an excuse to procrastinate!		plan planned
1699. Organize and set up a p____d procedure for work. Start at a definite t__e. Know exactly what it is you have to do, or learn, or accomplish. Don't wander aimlessly. Eliminate all excuses for procrastination.		planned time
1700. And keep this in mind: It is much simpler and much easier to org_____ and plan this way than the way you are doing things today!		organize
1701. All the preceding frames have been used to stress the main goal - to get down to w____ im- mediately, without a single moment of wasted effort.		work

1702. Most professional writers will tell you that they write for a certain number of hours <u>each</u> day. And they usually set a quota of a c___n number of words to get down on paper!		certain
1703. They sit down at the desk at a definite t___e each day.		time
1704. They allow no delays. Because they know that even a five minute d___y can kill an entire work period.		delay
1705. It's that ol' debil <u>'excuse'</u> again. The tendency will be to think, "Oh, what the heck, I wasn't able to get started on t___e anyway. I might as well do it tomorrow!"		time
1706. Excuses are a one-way street to pro- crastination and failure. Stay off that street. Start at a d_____te time each day.		definite
1707. As to your working conditions: A pro- fessional writer will have his typewriter at the same place and in the s___ position always. <u>Everything</u> he needs, ashtrays, cigarettes, pencils, erasers, glasses, paper, carbon, etc., <u>will be there</u>.		same
1708. Because everything he needs is already there, he will never have to get up after he's started - losing his train of thought or allowing <u>'ex___s'</u> to squeeze in.		excuses
1709. Be sure <u>your</u> working conditions are always set the way you <u>want</u> them. The best way to do this is to set them up properly, refill what has to be refilled, etc. - at the finish of the <u>preceding</u> day's w__k.		work
1710. On the other hand, I know one writer who breaks all his pencil points at the end of each day's work! This is a 'gimmick' he uses to help him to st__t the next day.		start

1711. At the right time the following day, he sees those pencils and has to start sharpening them. He has almost forced himself to s___t; he's already, at least, <u>thinking</u> of what he has to write.		start
1712. Association, remember? Those pencils must make him think of his writing, because one is ass_____d to the other!		associated
1713. If you can think of any similar 'gimmicks' to help you to get st____d, fine. Use them, if they work for <u>you</u>.		started
1714. All right – to help you to concentrate, you must first, above all, get down to w___.		work
1715. The easiest way to do this, is to ____. a) procrastinate b) sleep c) begin d) make excuses		c) begin
1716. You must have a p_____d procedure for any task which requires <u>concentration</u>.		planned
1717. Plan exactly what has to be done; start at the beginning; learn or do it step by step; know or p___ where you must st___ tomorrow!		plan start
1718. With this planned procedure or system, you have no time, reason or inclination for using _____. a) excuses b) paper c) pencil d) benzedrine		a) excuses
1719. Plan a definite time to st___ each day, and set a quota for the <u>amount</u> of w___ to be done.		start work

198

1720. Good, bad or indifferent, don't stop until that a_____ of work has been done!		amount
1721. Make it a rule never to d___y your starting time. Even a short delay can kill an entire working period.		delay
1722. Make sure the working conditions are right for you. Eliminate all possible chance for subconsciously or consciously making ex___s.		excuses
1723. If you follow these rules and suggestions for getting down to work consistently and con- scientiously, they will become h___ts.		habits
1724. Once you've formed the habit, getting down to work becomes instant and automatic. You're ready to slash into your w___ without any wasted time, motion or energy!		work
1725. Now let's look at the second step in c_____tion: How to concentrate exclusively on what you're reading or hearing.		concentration
1726. Concentration is exclusive attention on any one object or subject. Therefore the problem is, how do you give your entire and ex_____ att_____ to one subject?		exclusive attention
1727. Now we come to the real 'meat' of how to acquire the ability to con_____. There is one Golden Rule, one short phrase, I will teach you, which is the entire secret of concentration.		concentrate
1728. That Golden Rule is: GET YOURSELF INVOLVED!! Remember that and think about it. In order to give your exclusive attention to one subject, or to concentrate, you must get yourself in_____.		involved

1729. Now then, how do you get yourself _____d? Here's the 'Silver' Rule, the basic method and device for any form of thinking: ASK QUESTIONS!		involved
1730. I've touched on this in the section on creative thinking; and all thinking is basically the same. In any kind of thinking, you're trying to solve a p_____m.		problem
1731. If you think in the past, you're remembering; if you think in, or of, the future, you're anticipating or expecting, and if you think in the present, you're p_____m-solving.		problem
1732. At the moment, we're interested in the present; in problem-solving. To solve problems, you must ask _____ns.		questions
1733. I'll get to actual problem-solving in a little while - right now - concentration. The 'asking questions' device, which is used by scientists, inventors, businessmen, any one who has to con_____ or think, is the magic key to concentration.		concentrate
1734. It starts your thinking. I've already taught you to use this device for creative thinking. Now let's see how to apply it in order to c_____e on things you read.		concentrate
1735. All right; you have to read something, anything; technical matter, a homework assignment for school, etc. How do you concentrate on it; how do you get yourself in_____d?		involved
1736. Simply keep in mind that in any of these instances, you should read to find specific answers to s_____c questions.		specific
1737. Unless you are reading a novel or story simply for enjoyment, you are reading in order to find specific a_____s to specific q_____s.		answers questions

200

1738. So, before you <u>start</u> reading, ask yourself exactly what questions you want this article, book, magazine, lesson, newspaper, etc. to a____r.		answer
1739. List the questions on a piece of paper, if necessary. But <u>ask</u> the q_____s <u>first</u> – before you start reading.		questions
1740. Make up these questions by using those six serving men I mentioned in the idea-creating section, what, why, where, when, who and h__.		how
1741. For example, say you want to read an article on, "A Plan To Free Cuba." Here are some of the questions you may want a_____d. "<u>What</u> is the plan? <u>Who</u> is its author? <u>What</u> are his qualifications? <u>What</u> action does the plan require? <u>How</u> long would it take? <u>What</u> are its chances for success? <u>What</u> would happen if it succeeded?" and so on.		answered
1742. You are automatically in____d with the subject and with the material you're reading, simply because you are asking q_____s.		involved questions
1743. Do you see what this technique does for you? It centers your ex_____ att_____ on these important questions and prevents you from being <u>distracted by minor details</u>! And – you're <u>involved</u>.		exclusive attention
1744. Read with these questions in mind always. Every <u>sentence</u> you read must be judged on this basis: Does it answer your q_____s, or does it not?		questions
1745. Although this gets a bit into the area of speed-reading, which I'll touch on soon, if a sentence does <u>not</u> answer any of your q_____s, <u>flash read</u> it. That <u>is</u>, don't bother reading it word for word. Skim the sentence and continue searching for your answers.		questions
1746. If you have your particular q_____s in mind as you read, you will judge each sentence by whether it does or does not answer any of those questions.		questions

1747. If it doesn't, fl___ read that sentence; skim it. But, if it _does_ answer a question, follow this simple two-step procedure:		flash
1748. a) Slow down and read that s_____ce carefully. Be sure you understand it.		sentence
1749. b) Pick up your pencil and underline the key words of that s_____ce. That's right; mark up that book! Un_____ne the key words of the sentence that answers your question.		sentence Underline
1750. The key word idea is not new to you. You were taught how to locate them in the memory section on how to r_____r speeches; remember?		remember
1751. This underlining-the-k__ w___ technique is of utmost importance. It is a deliberate physical act which assures and insures the mental act of con_____n.		key word concentration
1752. It converts routine (and often boring) reading into active, physical thought; it prevents your mind from wandering. (And this, is another key to concentration; keep your mind from w_____ing.)		wandering
1753. It makes the material in any book or article come to life for you. It forces you to evaluate, weed out, judge and emphasize. It gets you completely in_____d!		involved
1754. You may underline only one or two sentences on an entire page, or, four or five in an entire article, because they are the only s_____ces that answer your specific questions.		sentences
1755. But, the less you u_____ne in an article, the better you should feel about it! Think of all the excess material, the padding, the unnecessary work you've eliminated!		underline

1756. If a sentence (or a paragraph) doesn't answer your question, it's worthless. So, all that remains for you to do now, is to glance over the article and concentrate on only the un_____ned sentences.		underlined
1757. All right then – what you're actually doing when you apply this technique is this: 1) You form q_____s. And 2) you read to a____r those questions. That's all there is to it!		questions answer
1758. You've just acquired a great step toward turning the reading of any material into your own personal acquisition. You've learned to c_____te on it as you hammer out your an___s.		concentrate answers
1759. The physical marks, the un_____ing of these an___s, will be your own personal milestones along the road to mastery of that material!		underlining answers
1760. They are an active, physical record of what you've learned. Ready to flash-review anytime you wish to go back over that material. They are also an active, physical step toward strengthening your con_____ing ability!		concentrating
1761. So; the Golden Rule for concentrating is: Get Y_____ Involved.		Yourself
1762. In order to get yourself involved – to give your exclusive attention to one subject – you apply the 'Silver' Rule: Ask _____s.		Questions

1763. Pre-questioning of any material you are about to read is the magic key to _____.
 	
    a) the door
    b) the car
    c) concentration
    d) the answer
		c) concentration

1764. Then, when you read that material, you are looking for sp___c answers to s_____ questions.		specific specific

1765. So, before you start reading, ask yourself the questions you want _____ .
 	
   a) eliminated
   b) concentrated
   c) hidden
   d) answered
		d) answered

1766. This technique centers your exclusive a_____n on the important issues and keeps your mind from w_____ing.		attention wandering
1767. If a sentence does not answer any of your questions, skim it. If it does answer a question, slow down and r___ that sentence slowly and carefully.		read
1768. Be sure you understand it. And, most important, pick up your pencil and underline that s____ce, or its key words.		sentence

1769. By doing this, you are getting yourself completely involved. You are actively asking questions and locating and _____ the answers.
   a) erasing
   b) reading
   c) underlining
   d) finding
		c) underlining

1770. The physical marks of underlining will be your milestones along the road to concentration and _____ of any material you're reading.
   a) mastery
   b) forgetting
   c) re-writing
   d) striving
		a) mastery

1771. Learn and apply these rules and suggestions on how to con_____ while reading, and it will make your concentration automatic!		concentrate
1772. Now let's apply the same technique of q_____n and a___r to listening!		question answer
1773. In addition to reading, we gain information from, and must learn how to c_____te on, things we hear.		concentrate

1774. Do you find it difficult to concentrate on speeches or lectures or even conversations? Well, the ability to concentrate while listening may be even more important than to do so while r__ding.		reading
1775. It is an indispensable art. That's right; it's not a natural gift, but an acquired art. You can acquire it by learning the rules set forth in the following frames. Basically, it is the same idea as con_____ing while reading.		concentrating
1776. The main problem is to be able to <u>maintain</u> <u>attention</u> while someone is talking or lecturing. Remember, you must give your exclusive attention, or m_____n attention on what the person is saying.		maintain
1777. It is, unfortunately, much <u>easier</u> to just allow your mind to wander. And, usually, you don't even realize that it <u>has</u> w____ed. When you do, it's too late; you've lost the speaker's train of thought.		wandered
1778. Let me tell you <u>why</u> it's easier to allow your mind to wander. The human brain thinks about four times as fast as the tongue can speak. That huge gap provides the time for all sorts of distracting personal thoughts; time for w____ing.		wandering
1779. There's only <u>one</u> way to avoid this mind-wandering; to fill in those time gaps; and to <u>con-centrate</u> – and that is to GET YOURSELF IN_____D!		INVOLVED
1780. Remember, that's the key to concentration! And you accomplish it in the same way as before, by self-q_____ing!		questioning
1781. Self-questioning will <u>force</u> you to keep pace with the speaker and to get in____d. It will do this in four different ways. I'll devote a few frames to these four ways so that you'll thoroughly understand the reasoning behind them.		involved
1782. First; by <u>summarizing</u> what the speaker has already said; trying to boil it down to a single thought or two. A__ yourself, "How can I sum up these statements in a single phrase or sentence? How and why do they tie in with his last point?" You're s____izing what the speaker has already said.		Ask summarizing

1783. Second; by anticipating the speaker's next point, with q_____s like, "What exactly is he getting at here? What examples will he give to prove this point? Where will he go from here?" and so on.		questions
1784. Ask yourself these questions and ant____te the answers. Anticipate the speaker's next point, and you're forcing yourself to stay with the subject and to concentrate.		anticipate
1785. Third; by listening between the lines for points that are not put into words. "What does he mean by that? Is he hinting at something he's not mentioning here? Why isn't he bringing up that point he mentioned last week?" etc. You're listening b____n the lines.		between
1786. Fourth; by asking yourself if you agree with the speaker! "Is that statement correct? Isn't he forgetting or neglecting to mention so and so? Doesn't he realize that that situation has altered?" and so forth. You're asking yourself whether you a____ with the speaker.		agree
1787. You are forcing yourself to keep pace with the speaker and to get i_____d with the subject by asking questions in these four main trains of thought.		involved
1788. You are summarizing what he's a____dy said; anticipating what he will say; listening b____n the lines and wondering whether you agree with him!		already between
1789. A tip to help you remember these four steps. There is an island in the Caribbean called, Saba. It is a mountainous island. Picture this island; picture Saba, and it will help you remember, summarize, a_____e, between (the lines) and do you agree!!		anticipate
1790. I've given some sample self-questions. You are to use your own, of course. Many of them will come to mind as you listen. Happily, you must l___n in order to ask yourself these questions.		listen
1791. These questions all have one vital trait in common. They change that listening from a passive to an active task! They eliminate mind-w_____ing.		wandering

1792. They <u>force</u> you to keep your mind constantly and <u>exclusively</u> focused on the sp_____'s thoughts; to literally pull the core of meaning from the speech, talk, lecture or conversation.		speaker's
1793. Basically, they <u>force</u> you to think step for step, along with the speaker! They <u>force</u> you to c_____te!		concentrate
1794. The ability to c_____ on what someone is saying is an indispensable art.		concentrate
1795. The main problem is to maintain att_____n while someone is talking or lecturing.		attention
1796. It is easy to let your mind wander because there is a large time gap between the speed of the human brain and the s___d of the human tongue.		speed
1797. The only way to avoid mind-wandering is to get <u>involved</u> and use the technique of ___ - _____. a) falling asleep b) taking milltown c) self-questioning d) hypnotizing yourself		c) self-questioning
1798. Ask questions in four ways. Remember the island of Saba. Summarize; anticipate; between the lines and do you _____ with the speaker.		agree
1799. <u>Summarize</u> what the speaker has already said; try to boil it down to one phrase or to a single th____t.		thought
1800. Anticipate the speaker's next point. Ask y_____f what he's getting at; is he going to prove it with examples, etc.		yourself

1801. Listen b____n the l___s for points he doesn't actually put into words. Is he hinting at something; what does he m___ by that, and so on.		between lines mean
1802. Do you agree with each point the speaker mentions? Is he c___ct? Has the situation changed on one particular point? Is he leaving out certain facts? and so on.		correct
1803. If you ask these questions, mentally, or in writing for a lecture, you're getting yourself i_____ with the speaker and his subject!		involved
1804. You're changing passive (or bored) listening to _____ participation and work. a) hazy b) active c) bored d) placid		b) active
1805. You're forcing your mind to cease its wandering and keep it constantly and with _____ _____ on the speaker's thoughts. a) much boredom b) exclusive attention c) maintained disinterest d) closed eyes		b) exclusive attention
1806. Make a habit out of these rules, suggestions and techniques and you'll have acquired the art of c_____ting while someone else is talking! --- Now let's go on to the fourth use of concentration. Let's explore the immensely profitable skills of problem-solving and decision-making --- and make you a master of each.		concentrating
YOU HAVE JUST COMPLETED COURSE #7 OF HARRY LORAYNE'S INSTANT MIND POWER TEACHING-MACHINE. COURSE #8 BEGINS ON THE NEXT SHEET.	No answer required. ↑	
	↑	
	↑	
	↑	
	↑	

COURSE #8: HOW TO MAKE PROBLEMS HALF-SOLVE THEMSELVES

1807. I've used one full previous section to help you to think creatively. All you learned there can be applied to <u>clear</u> thinking and c_____tion.		concentration
1808. As I told you before, thinking in the present is mainly <u>problem-solving</u>. So let's spend some time on learning how to concentrate directly on _____ - solving.		problem
1809. The first rule is the one you've already learned: Ask questions! Asking q_____s and tracking down the answers is the greatest single source of progress.		questions
1810. All the experiments going on in our scientific laboratories are nothing more than different and diversified ways of asking q_____s of nature. All inventions are really only physical answers to such questions.		questions
1811. A__ yourself continuously, "Why was, or is, a certain thing being done, or not done; and why was, or is, a certain method being used instead of another?" etc.		Ask
1812. You already know <u>how</u> to ask questions; just use those six honest serving men, what, why, when, ___, where and who!		how
1813. All right; rule one for solving p_____s is, ask questions. Unfortunately, few people who <u>think</u> they think, really do! <u>You must ask questions in order to think!</u>		problems
1814. Ask questions of y_____f and anyone else. Don't be afraid; remember, "He who asks a question is a fool for five minutes; he who doesn't ask a question remains a fool forever!"		yourself
1815. The second rule is: <u>Define Your Problem Precisely</u>! All the questions and all the answers in the world won't help, if you don't <u>really</u> know what the problem is. So, d___e the problem.		define

1816. Take any _____m and write it out in detail. When you try this, you'll find that many parts of the problem are really nothing but incidentals.		problem
1817. List only the essentials of the problem; keep eliminating the foggy un-essential details and you're getting down to the core of the _____.		problem
1818. Write down precisely WHAT is wrong – WHERE it is wrong – and WHY it is w____.		wrong
1819. Most problems well organized and pre-cisely d___ned in this way are already partially solved!		defined
1820. You may not realize it until you think about it, but many times we're concerned with problems that don't actually exist! Be sure the problem you feel you must solve – really e____s.		exists
1821. Then, do a little 'brainstorming!' List all the solutions you can, no matter how silly or wild. You realize that you're giving your exclusive _____, at that moment, to that problem and also to its solution.		attention
1822. You've eliminated all the fog surrounding the p_____ and you can give your attention and concentration to solving it.		problem
1823. Look for the key problem within the overall problem. Just to give one example; in building a bridge, the actual bridge construction is not the key p_____m! The ___ problem is the traffic that will be using that bridge.		problem key
1824. Where will that traffic be coming from and where will it be going to? How heavy will that traffic be at its peak time? How much heavier will that traffic get in years to come? The traffic is the ___ problem, not the bridge itself.		key

210

1825. All right; practice getting to the core or nucleus of any p_____ . Soon you'll be able to cut through the outside layers to the k__ problem inside. You'll be thinking of and attacking the disease not the symptom .		problem key
1826. Once the problem is whittled down to its essentials, to its k__ form, it is in a soluble and attackable form.		key
1827. Remember, the key problem is not always the obvious one! Any distant factors may contain that k__ you're looking for. Keep digging till you find it.		key
1828. Therefore, the second rule for concentrating on, and solving, problems is: D_____ the problem precisely! Cut away the non-essentials. Look for the k__ problem within the overall problem!		Define key
1829. The third rule is really an obvious one: <u>Get The Facts You Need To Solve That Problem!</u> The necessary tools for any type of thinking, are f___s.		facts
1830. You've got to develop the capacity for finding things out; for searching for facts. Almost any problem can be solved if you are aware of enough f___s about the situation.		facts
1831. Perhaps the best way of getting facts is to know <u>whom</u> to go to; whom to ask! Turn to experts and specialists in the particular field, if necessary, but g__ the facts!		get
1832. Let me give you one example. I know of an automobile dealer who hired an efficiency expert to find out why a certain percentage of the potential customers were walking out of the showroom <u>without</u> buying a car. He knew the p_____m. He was after the f___s.		problem facts
1833. Remember, the key problem was not the car itself, because other dealers were selling it well. The ___ problem was why weren't his salesmen scoring?		key

1834. I don't want to go into complete detail, but the efficiency expert found two apparently silly facts. Tie clips and clocks! All the salesmen wore the same large tie ___s with a model car on it; and there were many c___ks in the showroom.		clips clocks
1835. The expert suggested that both these things be eliminated! It seems that potential customers were becoming too interested in the ___ clips and were not giving their full attention to the sales pitch!		tie
1836. Also, in the process of being sold a car, too many potential customers would look at a cl__k, realize they were late for some appointment or other, and leave with a promise to return.		clock
1837. Of course, many of them never returned! They already had all the information; price, trade-in, model, etc., that they needed, so they perhaps bought from someone closer to them, etc. There are no more tie ___s or c___s in that dealer's showroom!		clips clocks
1838. I'm giving just this one perhaps extreme example of the importance of getting to the core of the problem. Get the f___s!		facts
1839. To help get those f___s and help solve the problem, we come to the fourth rule: Keep An Open Mind And Weigh All Sides Of The Problem!		facts
1840. Stop seeking justification for the action you want to take. Don't accept just those facts which fit your prejudices, and reject all others. Don't attempt to warp the f___s to fit your wish or desire.		facts
1841. Don't jump to false conclusions. For example, don't reason this way: "Joe Jones is a liar; Joe Jones is a politician; therefore all politicians are liars!" This is jumping to a false con_____n. Don't illogically substitute "all" for "some."		conclusion
1842. And always be sure your original assumption (or premise) is correct. For example: "Soups are always served hot; vichysoisse is a soup; therefore vichysoisse is always served hot." The original ass_____ (or premise) is incorrect.		assumption

212

1843. Soups are not always served hot. Vichy-soisse is a <u>cold</u> soup. So, be sure your original assumption on any thought or conclusion is a c____t one.		correct
1844. How can you avoid these pitfalls of incorrect thinking? The only way I can help you is by stressing the rule: <u>Keep an open mind and weigh all sides of the p____m.</u>		problem
1845. Consider every side of the problem <u>calmly and carefully</u>. That's the only way to keep <u>wish, sentiment and faulty thinking</u> from keeping you from the facts and from clouding and fogging your th____g.		thinking
1846. Finally, the fifth rule: <u>Let Your Thought Lead To Action!</u> Here is where we veer slightly away from the precise subject of c_____n and move more firmly into the p____m-s____g area.		concentration problem-solving
1847. In trying to solve any problem, be sure your thought leads to ac___.		action
1848. All the questions you ask, all the facts you collect, will be of little help if they, in turn, do not l___ to action.		lead
1849. After gathering all the facts and going through the self-questioning, you must come to a <u>decision</u>. Your first <u>act</u> is the reaching of a d____n.		decision
1850. <u>How</u> do you learn to make decisions? Well, the best advice I can give you is to work at <u>forming the habit</u> of making d____ns.		decisions
1851. Deliberate and weigh all the factors of the situation. List all the pros and all the cons. Let this act as a balance sheet or jeweler's scale. Your d____n, usually, should be made on the side toward which the heavier factors tip that scale.		decision

213

1852. A good idea is to devise two or more possible s_____ns or plans of action. Then d____e which is best - choose the best one.		solutions decide
1853. Do this by bringing all the factors to bear, as I just told you, on <u>both</u> solutions. Deliberate and weigh the evidence, facts, etc., of these two solutions and see which way that jeweler's s___ tips.		scale
1854. Just as one example: A manufacturer found that his product wasn't moving as well as usual because a competitor's product was displacing his. He arrived at three possible s_____ns.		solutions
1855. First, of course, was to develop a better product. Second, spend more money by increasing advertising and cut prices at the same time. And third, buy out the competitor. He had to make a d_____n; which was the best solution?		decision
1856. He made balance sheets on the three solutions. Listed the pr__ and c__s of each, like this:		pros cons
1857. The first possibility - developing a better product - wouldn't cost too much immediately. But it would involve long and tedious experiments; more delay as the competitor's pr____t kept displacing his; loss of clients, etc., etc.		product
1858. The second possibility - money spent on adv_____ing - would help his competitor too. Price cutting could start a price war he might not be able to win.		advertising
1859. The third possibility - buying out his competitor - involved a large immediate cash outlay. But there was an immediate gain of the net profits now being lost to the com_____r.		competitor
1860. If he bought out his competitor, he'd avoid an expensive battle, and so on. Of course, many, many more pros and c__s were listed.		cons

1861. After careful deliberation and weighing of these lists, or balance sh___s, it was obvious that the correct solution was to buy out the competitor.		sheets
1862. Once this d_____n was made, <u>action</u> was started!		decision
1863. Most problems do not entail decisions of that stature. Most decisions, after applying the rules – getting the facts and asking all the q_____s – can be made without all this lengthy deliberation.		questions
1864. Now, is there a way of assuring yourself that the decision you've made is the <u>right</u> one? Yes, there is. Here are two simple rules for checking out that d_____n.		decision
1865. First, if possible, <u>test out your decision on a small scale.</u> This, of course, is not always p_____le, but if it is, do so.		possible
1866. Second, assume that the d_____n has already been made unalterably. <u>Imagine yourself living with it;</u> anticipate the consequences, both immediate and years from now. Are you, and will you be, happy and satisfied with it?		decision
1867. Now do exactly the same thing with the choice you rejected. Your own experience and intuition will come to bear here, and in an almost eerie way, will help pinpoint the c____ct decision! Try it, you'll see that it works.		correct
1868. So, try to test out each s_____n on a small scale. And/or imagine the decision is already made, and try to forecast how it will come out.		solution
1869. Decision making is a habit. Apply the rules I've given you and ask these three questions of yourself over each decision. 1) Am I ready to use all the courage I have to back up this d_____n?		decision

1870.　2)　Do I have enough knowledge and experience of this subject to assure me that I'm making the c___ct decision?		correct
1871.　And 3), is this decision the best I'm capable of making? If your answer to each of these q_____s is affirmative, the odds are you've made the correct decision.		questions
1872.　If your a_____s are negative, do something about it! Keep working on the decision and the solution until the answers are affirmative.		answers
1873.　Practice on the small, or minor, decisions. Once you've formed the h___t of making them quickly and correctly, all you have to do is multiply in order to handle the big ones!		habit
1874.　Just remember, that the longer you take to make a d_____n, the closer you get to making no decision at all!		decision
1875.　Now, before we review all you've learned on concentration, let's do a quick review on concentration as particularly geared to problem-s___ing.		solving
1876.　Most thinking done in the _____ is concerned with problem-solving. 　　a)　future 　　b)　past 　　c)　present 　　d)　bathroom		c) present
1877.　The first rule for solving problems is: Ask q_____s.		questions
1878.　You must ___ questions in order to think.		ask

216

1879. The second rule is: D____ your problem precisely.		Define
1880. Write out the p_____ in detail and eliminate all the fog around it.		problem
1881. Learn to get down to the core or k___ problem.		key
1882. Most problems, well organized and precisely d____d are already partially solved.		defined
1883. Once the problem is whittled down to its key form, it is in a soluble and attackable form. Now, find the s_____n. Do a bit of <u>brainstorming</u> to help find that solution.		solution
1884. The third rule is: Get the f__s.		facts
1885. Turn to experts and specialists if necessary, but be sure you ___ the facts.		get
1886. The fourth rule is: Keep an open mind and weigh all factors of the p____m.		problem
1887. Don't distort the facts to fit your wish or d___res.		desires

217

1888. Be careful not to use exceptional cases as generalizations. Work with the <u>norm</u> rather than the ex_____n.		exception
1889. Make sure that your original assumption is correct. Look out for false or faulty thinking. Always check your original as_____n.		assumption
1890. Consider every element of the problem calmly and c___fully.		carefully
1891. The fifth rule is: Let your thought lead to a_____.		action
1892. Your first step toward action is to make a _____. a) problem b) solution c) prayer d) decision		d) decision
1893. Remember my rules for building good habits --- work at forming a h___t of making decisions.		habit
1894. Make up b____ce sheets for each solution. List all the pros and cons of each one. Your decision can then usually be based on those balance sheets.		balance
1895. To check if your decision is the correct one, try to test it out on a small scale; and/or imagine a decision already made. Then try to an_____te the consequences.		anticipate
1896. Finally, work until you get an aff____ve answer to these three questions. Am I ready to back up my decision? Do I have the knowledge and experience to assure a correct decision? And, is this decision the best decision I'm capable of?		affirmative

1897. Make it a habit to reach quick and correct decisions over minor problems and you'll solve larger p____ms much easier.		problems
1898. Now for a complete review on concentration. Let's look over everything we've learned in the last two courses. The first problem in concentration is to get down to w__k.		work
1899. Applicable here, is the third rule in the will power section; begin, and all its sub-rules. Stop pro_____ing.		procrastinating
1900. To help you to get down to work you must have a planned procedure. Set a definite t___ for sitting down to work each day.		time
1901. Know exactly what it is you have to do. Start at the beginning, and learn, or do, it step by s__. ,		step
1902. Don't delay your starting time or you'll set up ex____s for not starting at all.		excuses
1903. Be sure all working conditions are as perfect as possible. Get them ready after you finish the preceding day's w__k.		work
1904. Concentration is ex____ve attention on one subject.		exclusive
1905. The Golden Rule for concentration is: Get yourself in____d.		involved

219

1906. You get yourself involved by asking _____s.		questions
1907. When you read anything, you are looking for specific a_____s to specific questions.		answers
1908. As you read, look for answers. When you find an answer, pick up your pencil and un_____e the key words of that sentence.		underline
1909. This underlining–the–answer idea is of utmost importance. It forces you to weed out and evaluate. It gets you in_____d.		involved
1910. Be sure to apply this idea above all others; mark up that book, un_____ the sentence, or the key words of the sentence, that answers a q_____n!		underline question
1911. Concentrating while listening is an indispensable art. The main problem is to maintain att_____n.		attention
1912. You maintain attention by questioning what the speaker says. There are four ways of asking these q_____s. (Remember Saba.)		questions
1913. Summarize, ant_____te, listen b_____n (the lines), and decide if you agree with the speaker.		anticipate between
1914. Do this, and you're involved; you're changing passive listening into _____ participation. a) passive b) average c) active d) slovenly		c) active

220

1915. You're giving the subject your exclusive attention and your mind doesn't have the opportunity, time or inclination to w____r.		wander
1916. Most important on the subject of thinking and con_____n – and I can't stress this strongly enough – is to GET INVOLVED.		concentration
1917. The rules and techniques taught in this section are <u>all</u> geared to help you to do this one thing – get yourself _____.		involved
1918. Apply, practice and use all the techniques, ideas, hints and suggestions given here; ask questions, get involved – and you've acquired the art and the ability to c_____te. COURSE #9 BEGINS ON THE NEXT SHEET.		concentrate

COURSE #9: HOW TO FLASH-LEARN ANYTHING

1919. I don't think it's necessary for me to stress the importance of learning quickly, effectively and <u>rapidly</u> -- of absorbing new facts -- of growing in your business and social and intellectual pursuits. But rapid l_____g depends entirely on your ability to <u>read</u>.		learning
1920. The basic, fundamental skill required for all learning is reading. Effective r_____g and rapid l_____g go hand in hand.		reading learning
1921. The ability to study effectively, to keep pace with the steady stream of new innovations in any business or profession, depends almost entirely on your ability to r___ thoroughly, rapidly and with <u>understanding</u>.		read
1922. For example, doctors tell me that they receive probably twenty to twenty-five medical magazines monthly. And in order to really keep up, they <u>should</u> (although rarely do) r___ them all.		read
1923. If you don't r___ well, every written page becomes doubly difficult. You're forever doing extra and unnecessary work -- reading sentences over again; missing the meaning of certain passages; forgetting what you r___ the night before.		read read
1924. How do you read well? First of all, good reading is far <u>more than merely recognizing words</u>. Mechanical or passive reading is not enough. This p____ve and mechanical reading must be changed to <u>active</u>, aggressive reading!		passive
1925. Effective reading is far more than recognizing words. Effective reading is ac___e reading. It is taking those words and boiling them down into <u>thoughts</u>.		active
1926. That's right; effective reading is the art of boiling down dozens, hundreds, and even thousands, of words into <u>a few</u> vital th____ts.		thoughts
1927. Look at it this way; effective reading is a <u>search</u>. A s___ch for ideas, thoughts and <u>answers</u>.		search

1928. You must learn to get to the 'guts' of any reading matter quickly. This means you must separate the few really important th____ts from all the waste words and unnecessary details that surround them.		thoughts
1929. Therefore, the secret of effective reading is: First -- to <u>locate</u> main ideas, th____s and answers in the mass of words that contain them.		thoughts
1930. Second -- separate or spear each th____ out of all its unnecessary detail.		thought
1931. And third -- to <u>boil</u> each idea or th____t down to a few, easily-remembered words.		thought
1932. Since you're s___ching or hunting for these ideas and thoughts, the analogy of a spear-carrying hunter is not too far-fetched.		searching
1933. The man hunting for food must locate, spear and boil! So must you in order to read effectively. Lo____ the thought; sp___ it out of all that unnecessary detail and b__l it down to a few easily remembered words!		Locate spear boil
1934. You will learn to read effectively once you've mastered the techniques of locating, spearing and b___ng down.		boiling
1935. The remainder of this section will be devoted to teaching you to r___ and learn this new way.		read
1936. It will be devoted to teaching you these three things basically. First, how to set up the search for main ideas. How to glance over the reading matter in minutes and l____ the important thoughts <u>before</u> you begin to read.		locate

1937. Second, how to power-read. How to flash through page after page, sp____g those important thoughts and finishing in half the time it usually takes you.		spearing
1938. And third, how to b__l these main thoughts and ideas down to a few basic and easily remembered words.		boil
1939. Before going into the actual techniques, I want to stress that learning to read rapidly does not diminish your understanding of what you read. On the contrary, r___d readers are good readers.		rapid
1940. On the other hand, applying these rapid-learning techniques -- s___ching only for main ideas actually increases the speed with which you read.		searching
1941. Remember the three important things you have to learn; locate -- separate or spear -- and boil down. Let's take them one at a time. First; how to l_____ the important thoughts and ideas.		locate
1942. I'll start by teaching you to use this technique even before you start to r__dl		read
1943. When it comes to learning from reading matter; books, articles, etc., the biggest mistake most of us make is plunging right in and starting to read the first w__ds we see.		words
1944. This can be a crucial m___ke. It can cost you hours of wasted effort each time you have to read something.		mistake
1945. Starting to r__d that way is about the same as going on a car trip and taking the first highway you come to, without getting directions or studying a road map.		read

224

1946. The first thing you must learn to do when reading to learn, is get those directions, build that r___ map!		road
1947. Actually, it means applying exactly what this entire course is about -- organization. Here's how to go about it: Start by pre-reading whatever it is you have to r__d. Glancing over it before you begin to read it word by word.		read
1948. That's right: p__-read the material. A few moments applied be__e you actually begin to read, can save you hours later on.		pre before
1949. Exactly what do I mean by pre-reading? I mean gl_____g over that book, article, lesson, or what-have-you, and doing what I've been teaching you in the sections on creative thinking, concentration and p_____-solving. Look for answers to questions you've asked yourself!		glancing problem
1950. How do you find these q_____s (and answers) before you start reading? Most reading material already has certain signposts to help you do this.		questions
1951. These sign____s are chapter headings, section headings, table of contents, index, the foreword, etc. Plus any attention-drawing devices such as capital letters, underlinings, italics, and so forth.		posts
1952. Learn how to make use of these signposts, and you'll be able to pick out the main th_____ts of a book almost as quickly as you can turn the pages!		thoughts
1953. Let me touch first on the chief signposts, the ones you look for the first time you pick up a book. The s_____ts that will give you the 'guts' of that book in just a few minutes.		signposts
1954. The first one, of course, is the title. In most cases, a good title will give you, in a single phrase, the m__ theme of the book. It tells you, in a single phrase, what that b__k is going to do for you.		main book

1955. For example, the title of this programed course is INSTANT M___ P___ .		Mind Power
1956. This title tells you -- immediately -- that this course is going to improve your M___ P___ .		Mind Power
1957. Now -- you turn that title into a question. Before you read on, you ask yourself, "HOW is this course going to improve my M___ P___ ?		Mind Power
1958. This q_____n should automatically lead you to the table of contents.		question
1959. The table of c_____s takes the ultimate goal you're shooting for (How to improve your Mind Power), and breaks it down into a step for step process for you.		contents
1960. For example, our table of c____s shows you that you'll improve your Mind Power here by: 1) Improving your Memory. 2) Developing your Powers of Concentration . 3) Breaking Bad Habits. And so on.		contents
1961. If you study the table of contents, it immediately gives you an over-all outline of the b__k.		book
1962. After you study the t____ of contents, you know exactly what this book will give you. Now you simply read on to find out h___ you're going to improve your memory, develop your concentration, etc.		table how
1963. You've perhaps spent five minutes with the b__k. And you already know: 1) what it's going to do for you, and 2) how it intends to do it!		book

1964. From here on in, you'll actually be reading simply to answer the q_____s each of these chapter headings have raised in your mind.		questions
1965. I've just pointed out the two chief sign-posts of a book. The t___ itself and the table of c_____s.		title contents
1966. There are two more: 1) The <u>index</u>. And 2) the foreword or preface of the book. The i___x is a storehouse of minor topics of special interest to you.		index
1967. Glance over the in___ just to make sure certain points you're particularly interested in are there. Turn to one or two of the points and glance at them; don't bother reading them word for w___.		index word
1968. You'll get to them at the proper time and place; but now you know that they're <u>there.</u> That's important; to know that particular points or mater-ial you're interested in learning are th___!		there
1969. Finally, there's the foreword, preface or introduction to the book. R__d that next, before plunging into the main text.		Read
1970. This fore_____is the author's personal message to you. A brief outline of exactly where he is taking you and <u>how</u> he intends to get you there. By reading it, you will know in advance exactly what he is trying to accomplish.		foreword
1971. The f_____rd tells you what goals you are out to reach. And then the table of contents helps you to realize, step by step, exactly how you're going to reach them.		foreword
1972. All right, the four main signposts you have to check before you start reading are the title, the table of c_____s, the index and the foreword.		contents

1973. The <u>title</u> gives you, in one phrase, the _____ _____ of the book. a) page number b) main theme c) writing style d) author's earnings		b) main theme
1974. The t____ tells you, in a single phrase, what the book is going to do for you.		title
1975. The <u>table of contents</u> pinpoints the _____ between each of the chapters and the main theme of the book. a) pages b) questions c) relationships d) answers		c) relationships
1976. The t____ of c_____s thus shows you the steps by which you're going to accomplish your main goal.		table contents
1977. Glance at the <u>index</u> to see if certain particular points of information you're interested in are _____. a) there b) lost c) learned d) interesting		a) there
1978. The <u>foreword</u> is usually printed in front of the table of contents. Even if it isn't, read it first to get a brief outline of the book, and the _____ you're out to reach. a) bridges b) reasons (see next frame)	Your answer should go below ↓	
1978. (continued) c) heights d) goals		d) goals
1979. Apply these rules and suggestions and in one brief survey of any book, you know exactly what you want to get out of it and <u>where</u> it is l___ted.		located
1980. You have invested a short amount of time to glance over the book. In that short time you have picked out its main theme and its central th____ts.		thoughts

1981. You've built a skeleton or outline of that book; a <u>road map</u> to follow as you read. Now you'll have a lighted path to travel instead of stumbling along a dark path of confused jumbled w__ds.		words
1982. You've organized your reading! Now you can slash through that book or lesson with a definite purpose (a planned procedure) in mind. Without that purpose or p_____d procedure, you'd be wandering aimlessly.		planned
1983. In this short preview, you have acquired a better grasp of the r__ding matter than if you just read aimlessly for hours. You have <u>direction</u>.		reading
1984. You can now read each individual chapter in chronological order, with perfect understanding of how it ties into the chapter that has gone before it, the ch____r that follows it, and the main theme of the book as a whole.		chapter
1985. You're now ready to read the text itself. You're ready to cut through to the heart of its main th____ts and ideas almost as quickly as your eyes move down the page.		thoughts

1986.   The same exact signpost technique -- applied now to <u>individual</u> <u>chapters</u> -- can mine this information for you, in almost a single 'glance-through.' So look for the _____ first.
          a) words
          b) signposts
                         (see next frame)
	Your answer should go below ↓	

1986. (continued)
 	
          c) letters
          d) pages
		b) signposts

1987. What you'll actually be doing, <u>after</u> you've mastered this technique, will be to practically 'scan-read' each individual ch____r, quickly, easily and with complete <u>understanding</u>.		chapter
1988. You'll 'flash' read; skim; separate the main th____ts from the unnecessary detail.		thoughts

1989. How do you apply the 'signpost' technique to each individual chapter? The same way you applied it to the entire book. Except it's pinpointed even more. There are more sign____s.		signposts
1990. Actually, there are five signpost parts; some of which you'll find in any individual ch_____.		chapter
1991. Let's take them one by one and see how they'll help spear the main ideas right out of each chapter <u>before</u> you actually begin to r__d the text.		read
1992. I probably won't have to spend more than one or two frames on each, since you already have the basic idea of how to locate and use the s_____st parts. And you will not have to utilize all of them; just the ones that are necessary, as you'll see.		signpost
1993. First, of course, is the chapter <u>title</u>. Just as the title of the book itself tells you what the entire book is about, the chapter t_____ tells you what the chapter is about. What it includes and does not include.		title
1994. The chapter t____ immediately tells you the main theme of each chapter.		title
1995. This leads you to the second chapter s_____st -- the <u>section headings</u>. They are separated from the text, and set in bold type.		signpost
1996. These s_____ headings break down the chapter into its main ideas. Reading them quickly, without the intervening text, gives you an outline or skeleton of the chapter.		section
1997. Of course, if the book you're going to read <u>has</u> no section h_____s, just go on to the third chapter signpost -- the <u>paragraph heads</u> or <u>bold prints</u>.		headings

1998. These p_____h heads are <u>not</u> separated from the rest of the paragraph, but <u>are</u> set in bold type. They boil the main topic of <u>each</u> paragraph into a single phrase or sentence for you.		paragraph
1999. By reading these p_____ heads quickly, without reading the rest of the paragraphs, you again get the main thoughts of the chapter in a flash.		paragraph
2000. Now for a different type of chapter s_____t, the <u>introductory paragraphs</u>. Here, in the first paragraph or two of each chapter, the author tells you what to look for in the text that follows.		signpost
2001. He gives an introduction to the ch____r and ties it to the chapters that preceded it.		chapter
2002. Thus, the in_____ry paragraph usually boils down the main thought or thoughts in the material of that chapter <u>for you</u>.		introductory
2003. When you are finished with the in_____ paragraphs, the next thing to check is the <u>summary</u> or closing paragraphs at the end of the chapter. These are the author's last words on that ch____r.		introductory chapter
2004. They are his own outline or skeleton of the material covered in the chapter. This summary or cl____g paragraph tells you what the <u>author</u> deems important, in that chapter.		closing
2005. Therefore, these final words deserve careful study <u>before</u> you begin to actually r__d the text.		read
2006. Now -- please keep in mind that this entire pre-reading technique is essentially a <u>search</u>. You're s_____ing for the main thoughts of each chapter.		searching

2007. This search gives you a quick outline of the ch____r and tells you exactly what you're looking for and exactly where to find it.		chapter
2008. This search begins with the chapter title and continues with each of the other s____st parts until you've uncovered the main ideas of that ch____.		signpost chapter
2009. Therefore, you DO NOT have to check all the chapter s_____s in each chapter. You check only enough signposts to give you the main th____s. Then you ignore the others.		signposts thoughts
2010. For example, with many books, just glancing at the chapter title and the section h____gs, could be quite enough to give you the main ideas.		headings
2011. Then you'd go right into the actual reading of that chapter text without bothering with the other signpost p__s of the chapter.		parts
2012. With a minimum of practice, this pre-r___ing, quick-survey technique will not only give you the main idea of a ch____ in one glance-through, but will prepare you for reading and really learning and absorbing it.		pre-reading chapter
2013. The first two chapter signposts are the chapter title and section h____gs.		headings
2014. Following these are, the introductory p_____phs and then the s____y or closing paragraphs.		paragraphs summary
2015. And finally -- the p_____h headings.		paragraph

2016. All right; you've learned how to pre-read the chapter and to locate and spear out those main th____s. But your knowledge of the chapter is, of course, still incomplete.		thoughts
2017. Now you have to read the text itself to find out exactly what you should know about each of those m___ ideas.		main
2018. Again, before starting to read, how do you tell exactly what it is you should know about each main thought you've just located? Simple; use that self-q_____ing technique I've already taught you!		questioning
2019. Just turn each of those important ideas into a q_____n by placing a what, why, where, when, who or how, in front of it!		question
2020. Use these 'six tiny keys to knowledge' to form q_____s out of the main thoughts, and then simply read the text to find the answers!		questions
2021. Now, if you've applied what you've learned so far, you've pre-read a new chapter in three simple and logical steps. First, you've checked the chapter s____sts.		signposts
2022. Second, you've used those signposts to spear the main i___s and thoughts out of that chapter.		ideas
2023. And third, you've turned those main ideas into q_____ns.		questions
2024. Now you simply read the text to answer those q_____s.		questions

2025. But -- you won't realize how quickly you can do this, until you've actually practiced and applied this p__-r___ing technique.		pre-reading
2026. This pre-reading, quick-survey, question and a____r technique is one of the most powerful tools of reading you'll ever acquire. Practice it until it becomes second nature; until you're an expert at it!		answer
2027. You can use it for any piece of material you read. Do so, and it will eventually cut your r___ing time in half, and more important, you will double the amount of learning. And remembering!		reading
2028. Now we come to one last technique while you are power-reading the actual t_xt. You've already learned it in the section I devoted to concentration.		text
2029. I suggest you refer back to the section on c_____n; particularly that part of it that teaches concentration as you read.		concentration
2030. Because after you've checked the chapter signposts; speared out the m___ ideas and turned them into q_____s; you're ready to read the actual text exactly as I taught you in the section on how to concentrate while reading.		main questions
2031. Just as a very fast review; Remember that the main points you're looking for have been turned into questions. You are now reading in order to find specific a____s to specific questions.		answers
2032. If a sentence does not answer a question, skim it. If it does answer a question, slow down and read that s____ce carefully.		sentence
2033. Be sure you understand it and then, that single important physical act, underlining (remember?) the sentence or the key words of that s_____.		sentence

234

2034.　These physical marks, the un_____ing of the answer to your questions are the milestones along the road to mastery of any material you read.		underlining
2035.　So -- if you've applied the entire pre-reading technique properly -- the actual reading of the chapter, including the un_____ng becomes incredibly fast and easy!		underlining
2036.　During this actual reading, you'll be skimming over about 85% of the text, searching only for the answers to your main q_____s.		questions
2037.　As you actively underline each an___ to a main-thought question, you are absorbing it better because of the action. And, you're creating a list of key words by which you can later remember the chapter.		answer
2038.　You can either use my Link method of memory as you've been taught, or, if it is an educational assignment you're reading, list the under___ed words, the answers, in your notebook so that you always have the outline. Or both!		underlined
2039.　All right then! _____ reading is more than merely recognizing words; it is the art of boil-ing many words down to a few main thoughts. 　　a) Sad 　　b) Sloppy 　　c) Effective 　　d) Remedial		c) Effective
2040.　Basically, effective reading is a _____ for ideas, thoughts and answers. 　　a) package 　　b) reason 　　c) search 　　d) caution		c) search
2041.　The secret of effective reading is to first: _____ the main thoughts, in the mass of words that contain them. 　　a) locate 　　b) forget 　　c) write 　　d) create		a) locate
2042.　Step two is to spear or _____ each thought you've located. 　　a) kill 　　b) wound 　　c) fish 　　d) separate		d) separate

2043. And, step three, is to ____ each located and separated thought or idea down to its most easily remembered words.
    a) sit
    b) boil
    c) lacerate
    d) read
		b) boil

2044. Start to apply this technique of pre-r_____g to the entire book before you begin to read a single word of it.		reading
2045. Build a road map to follow, by using these four signposts: the title, the table of _____s, the foreword or introduction and the index of the book.		contents
2046. Once you've applied the p___-r____ng technique to the book itself, you know just what you want to get out of it and where it is located.		pre-reading
2047. You then apply the same technique to each individual chapter. There are five possible signpost parts to look for and use. First is the chapter t____.		title
2048. Not necessarily in this order, the chapter title is followed by the s_____n headings, the p_____ph heading or bold print and the introductory paragraphs.		section paragraph
2049. Also, you can utilize the s_____y paragraph.		summary
2050. It is not necessary to use all the chapter s_____t parts. Check only enough signpost parts to give you the main ideas of the chapter.		signpost
2051. Once you've applied the pre-reading technique to each individual chapter, you're ready for the self-q_____g technique. Turn the ideas into questions.		self-questioning

236

2052. Now, you simply read the actual text to find the an____s to those questions.		answers
2053. And, you now can power-read that text by skimming what does not answer a question and un_____g what does!		underlining
2054. You have learned the fantastic technique, and gained the important ability, to pre-read and po___r-read!		power-read
2055. Locate, separate and boil down! That's the simple secret of eff_____ reading.		effective
2056. May I stress that if you practice these techniques, you have acquired the most powerful tool there is for rapid reading and rapid and effective l_____g!		learning
2057. Special Note For Slow Readers: I do want to point out what I call the "motion-sickness" of slow reading. Hand motion, lip motion and head m_____n.		motion
2058. These are habits that slow readers picked up during their school years and haven't been able to b___k. If you point out the words as you read with finger or pencil, that slows you up.		break
2059. Basic reading should be done with the eyes only! if you're a 'pointer', break that habit! Practice reading with your hands folded tightly in your lap. Do that until you see that it is not necessary to p____t out the words.		point
2060. Next time you're reading, notice if your lips are moving. If they are, you're slowing up your reading pace. You're slowing reading speed to speaking s___d.		speed

2061. Break that h___t! Try biting on a pencil as you read, until you do!		habit
2062. Finally, try not to move your head from side to side as you read. This is both tiring _and_ it slows up your reading. Only your eyes should move. Only your e_ s need to move!		eyes
2063. Each time you catch yourself moving your head from side to read, stop it. Keep _on_ stopping it until you've br___n the habit.		broken
2064. If necessary, place your open hands to the sides of your head and hold tight as you read. This will keep you from both pointing _and_ m____g your head from side to side.		moving
2065. If you have to, bite a pencil at the same time! You may look silly, but you'll cure your reading 'm____n-sickness'!		motion
YOU HAVE NOW COMPLETED COURSE #9 OF HARRY LORAYNE'S INSTANT MIND POWER TEACHING-MACHINE. COURSE #10 BEGINS ON THE NEXT SHEET.	No answer required.	
	↑ ↑	
	↑ ↑	
	↑ ↑	

COURSE #10: HOW TO MAKE ONE HOUR DO THE WORK OF TWO		
2066. <u>The effective use of time</u> is probably one of the most important parts of organization you can (see next frame)	No answer required.	
2066. (continued) acquire. Plutarch said, "The greatest of all sacrifices is the sacrifice of t____ .		time
2067. There is no question that this is one respect in which we're all created equal. Nobody has more time than you have and nobody has less t____ .		time
2068. No one can inherit time, or keep it in a bank to accumulate interest. One hour contains sixty minutes no matter who is using that h__r.		hour
2069. And no matter who you 'know', you can't get more than twenty-four hours in any one day. I guess the only way to <u>save</u> t ___ is to <u>spend</u> it wisely!		time
2069A. <u>Spend</u> your ____ wisely and you're <u>saving</u> time.		time
2069B. I'm sure you're always complaining that you don't have enough ____ to do all the things you want to.		time
2070. <u>Most</u> of us nowadays are complaining about never having enough time. Well, I can't agree. You <u>do</u> have e____h time if you learn how to use it properly and effectively.		enough
2071. Usually, the busiest people have time for anything. There's an old saying that goes, "If you want something done quickly, give it to a man who is too b__y to do it."		busy

2072. He'll find time for it because he can't afford to let the chores mount up. And, of course, the busy man has usually learned to economize and org___ze his time. To him, time is too valuable to handle wastefully.		organize
2073. Organization is essential in order to use time effectively. If you 'never' have time for anything, you are just not org_____ing properly.		organizing
2074. I have already discussed the time-consuming habit of indecision. Since I feel that ind_____n is the _most_ time-consuming of habits, it deserves another mention or two.		indecision
2075. If you apply the rules and hints I've already given you, you will break that habit. Just keep in mind that you're usually better off making mistakes than not making d_____ns.		decisions
2076. That's right! If your d_____n is the wrong one, it can most likely be corrected. If you made the wrong choice, you'll know it soon enough, and you can switch to the better choice. At least you won't have to decide any more.		decision
2077. But make your choice now. Take the first step in any direction. Once you start, you'll at least get something d__e!		done
2078. Of course, important decisions may require time and thought. It's those small, really inconsequential decisions that you may waste too much valuable t___ on.		time
2079. Questions like these: Should I take a cab or bus; plane or train? Should I buy this one, or the one that costs a couple of dollars more? And so on. Why waste t___ making momentous decisions over small things?		time
2080. Here's a little 'trick' that may save you countless minutes. First of all, if you have a ch___ce between two small things where no money is involved, do the thing that's easier for you; the one that requires less effort; then forget it. It's as simple as that!		choice

2081. Where small amounts of money are involved, do this: Settle on an amount that's really unimportant to you. For example, make up your mind once and for all, that you will look upon any a____t up to $5.00 with indifference.		amount
2082. Now, whenever that amount, or less, is involved -- again, do the thing that's easier for <u>you</u>! Once you can make yourself believe that the a____t (whatever you decide on) is inconsequential, there is no longer any need to waste time deciding.		amount
2083. Is the difference in money between the cab and the bus less than $5.00? If it is, and that's the amount you decided is incon_____l, take a cab! No need to bother deciding over two items if the difference is $ 5.00 or less any more -- buy the better one, etc.		inconsequential
2084. Indecision is the most time-consuming of habits. You're usually better off making m____kes than not making decisions.		mistakes
2085. When it comes to small things, make a choice <u>now</u>. Do <u>something</u> and get it off your mind; use the t___ saved for more important things.		time
2086. Decide on an amount of money which you consider unimportant. Any choice involving that amount or less can be decided instantly. Do the thing that's e____er for <u>you</u>! ·		easier
2087. All right, you've learned rule #1 for using t___ effectively; form the habit of <u>deciding about little things instantly</u>! Now let's go on to our second rule.		time
2088. Are you always way behind in your duties or chores? If you are, I can only suggest that you're attempting to do too much or you're not org____ing your time efficiently or properly.		organizing
2089. A rule to help you to do this is: <u>Make a Plan For Each Day</u>! Simply make a p___ for each day and you'll <u>gain</u> time.		plan

2090. Make your plan for each day and <u>commit</u> yourself to it; <u>put it in writing</u>! Just a few sentences on a scratch pad will do; but c ____ t yourself to that plan in writing.		commit
2091. Then stick to that plan as closely as you can. Of course, you must always leave some unscheduled time for emergencies. Some flexibility in your plan is essential; but <u>unlimited</u> fl_____ty only wastes time!		flexibility
2092. Not only will this idea help you to organize your time more efficiently; it is also a good self-motivator. Planning to meet goals and objectives and to do certain things at certain times are good self-m_____rs.		motivators
2093. In all cases, try to form your goals clearly in your mind. Until your g____s are decided on, it's difficult to plan. So decide on specific goals for each day (or week).		goals
2094. Once your goals are clear, your planning is simply the determination of <u>actions</u> which will lead to the attainment of those g____s.		goals
2095. When you make your plan, you're actually deciding in advance what, when, where and how those a_____ns are to be taken.		actions
2096. So; rule #2 for organizing your time more efficiently is: Make a _____ for each day.		plan
2097. Now I want to give you some sub-rules to aid you in applying these two main rules. The two main rules are; form the habit of de___ding over the little things instantly; and, make a p___ for each day.		deciding plan
2098. An effective guide for approaching routine work is this: Concentrate on doing one thing at a time! It is difficult to con _____te on more than one thing at a time.		concentrate

2099. Do one job or chore; <u>finish</u> it; then go on to the next one. If you attempt to do too much at once, every job you're working on, every goal you're working toward, will suffer, and more t____ will be consumed and wasted.		time
2100. Now, <u>which</u> chores do you do first? Well, you've got to use a bit of judgment here. Ordinarily, I would suggest that first you do the ch____s that can <u>wait</u>, <u>then</u> do the urgent ones.		chores
2101. In this way, you're applying my 'backing yourself into a corner' technique! You've <u>got</u> to take care of the ur____t things; they'll get done anyway.		urgent
2102. It's those items that can wait, that usually <u>do</u> wait and wait, and sometimes linger on in your mind for weeks and months. They aggravate your indecision, hold up your work, and waste precious t____ .		time
2103. So do these f___t! You'll be amazed at how much more you'll get accomplished. When you know there are urgent duties awaiting you, the minor ones will get done faster. Otherwise, they take too much of your valuable time.		first
2104. You see, usually "work expands so as to fill the time available for its completion." If you had only minor chores to do, without the urgent ones waiting, you'd take that much more time to do the m____r ones.		minor
2105. If you always tackle the important jobs first, the minor necessary ones may never get done. Do the ones that c__ wait first.		can
2106. The exception to the rule of doing the things that can wait first is when you're faced with a choice of several tasks including some that <u>worry</u> you. In that case, it's best to take care of the ones that w____y you first.		worry
2107. When you're w_____d and anxious, your effectiveness may suffer, so start with the task that's preying on your mind; take care of the trouble and conflict first.		worried

2108. In this way, you'll be better able to undertake and complete the other duties and chores. Your eff_____ness will not be impaired because of particularly worrisome tasks.		effectiveness
2109. So you see, you have to use your own judgment. Ordinarily, do the things that can wait first, except when faced with tasks that w_____ you.		worry

2110.   Then, get the ones that worry you off your mind _____ .
    a) last.
    b) forever.
    c) first.
    d) easily.
		c) first.

2111. In any case, avoid spending so much time preparing for work that there's no time left to <u>do</u> the w___k.		work
2112. <u>Too</u> much time spent in planning may leave too little time for putting those p____s into action! I think as in most anything else, you must learn to reach a happy medium.		plans
2113. A rule that many busy executives use, and which can apply to anyone who is 'over-correspondenced' and/or always short of t____ is: Handle <u>any</u> correspondence or paper only <u>once</u>!		time
2114. This has been called the 'million dollar' idea. Make it a rule and you'll save valuable hours. Handle any correspondence or paper only o_____ .		once
2115. It requires practice and will power and you may never apply it to perfection, but after enough pr_____ce, you may come close to perfection.		practice
2116. And, whether you do or not, just <u>trying</u> to a___ly this rule will gain precious time for you each day. Any letter you receive, answer it or discard it <u>right at that moment.</u>		apply

2117. If you're an executive, when you receive a piece of correspondence, delegate it immediately to a subordinate who can handle it. Every time a piece of c_____nce goes through your hands more than once, you're wasting time.		correspondence
2118. This is basically the standard 'do it now' way of thinking. Make this a h____t and you _must_ save time.		habit
2119. Speaking of h___t, another essential technique for organizing your time is to make routine chores, things you do all the time, habitual or automatic.		habit
2120. You've already done so in many instances. Brushing your teeth or shaving or winding the clock, etc. These are h_____ual actions; you've time to think of other things while you're doing them.		habitual
2121. This may seem petty to you; but it's amazing how much time you'll save if you can do that with all small and repetitive chores. Re-read my section on how to acquire good h____ts.		habits
2122. Apply those rules to all the minor and re_____ve chores until they become habits, and you'll be gaining time.		repetitive
2123. Try to make it a h____ to put things in the same place all the time. You'll save hours because you won't have to search for things too often.		habit
2124. An excellent time-saving habit to get into is: _Start things on time!_ This h____ alone will save you hundreds of hours per year!		habit
2125. A little procrastination goes a long way in eating up that precious time. "Lose an hour in the morning and you'll be all day seeking that h____ !" Don't allow chores to overlap.		hour

2126. Start things on t___ . It's really just as easy to get out of bed the first time the alarm rings as it is to set it for five or ten minutes later.		time
2127. Another good rule to apply for using time more efficiently is the 'cushion' rule. The television industry, where time is of utmost importance, has been using this c_____n idea since its inception.		cushion
2128. They always leave a 'cushion' of time for every program. This is to allow for any accidents, or for any part of a show that takes a little more t___ than originally planned.		time
2129. Why not use the same idea? Make it a habit to allow a little more time than you think is neces- sary for any particular task. Leave yourself a c_____.		cushion
2130. If you think a certain chore will take an hour, allow yourself an h____ and fifteen minutes at least.		hour
2131. If the chore <u>does</u> take only an hour, you can start your next one earlier, and have the c_____n at the beginning of the next job.		cushion
2132. Use this idea when you make your plan for the day. Plan the day with '_____ns' of time.		cushions
2133. Do so and you'll rarely have to suffer that breathless, rushed feeling. And; you'll probably wind up saving an hour or more each day. These extra h____s can then be used for those things you 'never have time for'.		hours
2134. All right; we all have the same amount of time. The important thing is whether we _____ it wisely. a) lose b) remember c) forget 246 d) spend		d) spend

2135. In order to use time effectively, _____ is essential. a) speed b) a clock c) organization d) patience		c) organization
2136. One of the most time-consuming habits is, _____. a) organization b) indecision c) sleeping d) speed		b) indecision
2137. In most cases, you're better off making _____ than not making decisions. a) coffee b) time c) mistakes d) plans		c) mistakes
2138. Make a choice now; get started and involved and you'll get something done. Then you won't have to make any further d_____ns on that subject.		decisions
2139. Set an amount of money you consider unimportant; and when a decision involves that amount or less, do the thing that's _____ for you. a) faster b) easier c) slower d) greater		b) easier
2140. So rule #1 for using time effectively is: Form the habit of deciding over the little things _____. a) slowly b) twice c) instantly d) carefully		c) instantly
2141. Rule #2 is: Make a _____ for each day. a) plan b) hourglass c) survey d) gain		a) plan
2142. Put the plan in writing. _____ yourself to the plan. a) Chain b) Bring c) Sign d) Commit		d) Commit
2143. Planning to meet g____s and objectives is a good self-motivator.		goals

2144. A sub-rule for organizing your time is: Con _____e on doing one thing at a time.		Concentrate

2145. Do one job at a time; _____ it; then go on to the next one.
    a) love
    b) hate
    c) finish
    d) forget
		c) finish

2146. Except in cases where you have tasks waiting that are <u>worrying</u> you, do the chores that <u>can</u> wait _____.
    a) last
    b) first
    c) third
    d) later
		b) first

2147. If you do, you're using the 'backing yourself into a corner' technique. The ur____t tasks manage to get done; the ones that can wait, do wait.		urgent

2148. If a chore is preying on your mind, do <u>that</u> one first so that your effectiveness is not _____.
    a) impaired
    b) noticed
    c) sharpened
    d) organized
		a) impaired

2149. Another good sub-rule to follow is: Handle any correspondence or paper only o____.		once
2150. Decide on the answer to a letter <u>then</u>; don't leave it lying around to prey on your mind and to waste t____ .		time

2151. Try to make routine and repetitive chores automatic and/or _____ .
    a) easy
    b) difficult
    c) habitual
    d) scarce
		c) habitual

2152. An important sub-rule is: _____ things on time.
    a) Find
    b) Plan
    c) Say
    d) Start
		d) Start

2153. Stop restricting yourself to exact amounts of time. Use the '_____' idea. a) cushion b) pillow c) clock d) counting		a) cushion
2154. Tenseness, lateness and disappointments can easily be avoided if you use the c_____ idea.		cushion
2155. Use the cushion idea when you make your written plan for the day. Simply plan and org_____e your time to meet the requirements of any given activity --- and you might even add 10% for emergencies!		organize
2156. As in everything else I've taught you so far, you _must_ try, apply and _use_ these rules and suggestions. Do so, and you'll immediately start or_____ing your time.		organizing
2157. Benjamin Franklin once said, "Dost thou love life? Then do not squander t____ , for that is the stuff life is made of."		time
YOU HAVE NOW COMPLETED COURSE #10 OF HARRY LORAYNE'S INSTANT MIND POWER TEACHING-MACHINE. **COURSE #11 BEGINS ON THE NEXT SHEET.**	No answer required.	

COURSE #11: HOW TO DEVELOP "X-RAY" POWERS OF OBSERVATION

2158. At the beginning of this programed learning course, I taught you how to start t____ning your memory.		training
2159. You were taught that a trained memory is based on association. But, before you can ass____te _anything_, that thing must be _observed_.		associate
2160. Shakespeare once wrote, "It is the disease of not listening, the malady of not marking, that I am troubled withal." He was talking about ob_____tion.		observation
2160A. A trained memory is based on association _and_ ob____tion.		observation
2160B. You cannot remember _anything_ if you do not _____ it first.		observe
2160C. "Listening and marking" _means_ obs___ing.		observing
2161. The memory systems I taught you are actually based on exactly that: l____ning and marking. They _force_ you to observe without pain.		listening
2162. As I told you then, you cannot form a Substitute Word for a name, or find the outstanding feature on a face, without first really listening to (observing) the ____ , or marking, looking at (observing) the ____ .		name face

2163.   You cannot associate or remember anything if you do not _____ it first.
    a) forget
    b) observe
    c) write
    d) decipher
	b) observe

2164. Unfortunately, too many of us see, but rarely really observe. And; seeing means little, observation everything. The only thing you can do about sharpening your sense of observation is to practice being ob____ant.	observant
2165. If you think you do have a sh___p sense of observation, let me prove that you probably don't. Try to answer these questions: In which direction do you turn the key to open your front door?	sharp
2166. What is the exact balance in your check book? Which two letters of the alphabet are not on a dial telephone? Have you ever ob____ved which light is usually on top of the traffic light, red or green?	observed
2167. If you've a _____red correctly so far, try these: Is the #6 on your wrist watch dial the Arabic #6 or the Roman Numeral VI? What brand of cigarettes does your best friend smoke? What color socks are you wearing right now?	answered
2168. All these questions are pertaining to things you've seen many times; if your answers are incorrect, you've never ob_____d them.	observed
2169. PARIS IN THE THE SPRING X Look at this box for a moment. What does it say? Does it say, "P____ in the spring"?	Paris
2170. PARIS IN THE THE SPRING X Look at it again. Do you still think it says, "Paris in the spring"? If you do, you're like most people; you're not ob_____ing accurately.	observing
2171. PARIS IN THE THE SPRING X Look again, and point to each word as you read it. Now; do you see? It says, "Paris in the the spring". There is an extra ___ in the phrase!	the

2172. Well, now you know that to just look or see is easy, but to observe accurately is an art. It is an ___ and a skill that can be acquired.		art
2173. In the business world, it's observation that yields money-making and m___y-saving improvements and ideas.		money
2174. The effectiveness of all actions, in business <u>and</u> social life, depends to a large extent on your capacity for sharp, thorough and accurate ob_____n.		observation
2175. All right; to put it basically, we see with our eyes, but <u>observe</u> with our minds. The ability to observe accurately is part of m___d organization.		mind
2176. Accurate observation is not simple, nor can it be achieved without a bit of effort. Like most everything else in this course, however, it can become a h___t if you practice it consciously and ·conscientiously.		habit
2177. Observation implies a <u>clear mental picture</u> of what is seen. It requires the seeing of <u>detail</u> and the realization that a complete picture is composed of many d_____ls.		details
2178. How do you get a clear mental p_____re of what you see? Well, to bring it down to basics again, the difference between seeing with your eyes only and observing with your mind is -- <u>attention</u>.		picture
2179. The first, and really the only, rule for sharpening your sense of observation is: <u>Pay Attention!</u> Observation equals seeing <u>plus</u> awareness. This is brought about by att_____n.		attention
2180. All the rules and suggestions that I gave you in the sections on concentration, will power, creative thinking and habits, are applicable here. They are the rules that teach you about 'exclusive attention'; or, as I prefer in this case, <u>focused</u> att_____n.		attention

2181. If you have learned to apply exclusive or f____ed attention as I've already taught you, then you're already on the way toward learning to observe accurately.		focused
2182. Many years ago, Publilius Syrus said, "The eyes are blind when the mind is elsewhere". So remember, your eyes see only what you l___ for.		look
2183. Therefore, you must learn to make it a habit to keep in mind what it is you're l___king for at all times.		looking
2184. The first, and really the only, rule for sharpening your sense of observation is: ___ _____ . a) don't look. b) pay up. c) pay attention. d) fall asleep.		c) pay attention.
2185. When you look at <u>anything</u> with _____ attention, you <u>must</u> be observing it; it is <u>registering</u> on your mind. a) focused b) sloppy c) faulty d) wavering		a) focused
2186. Now, although paying attention is really the only rule, there are some sub-rules, and also some pitfalls to beware of. Beware of observation distortion due to personal interest. What you observe is mostly determined by what <u>you</u> are in_____d in.		interested
2187. Many people will look at, or see, the same thing and pay attention and observe only segments of it. They'll observe only the segments that they're i_____d in.		interested
2188. So, how well you observe <u>accurately</u> is determined by <u>interest</u> and training. To be interested, apply the rules I gave you in the section on creative th___ng.		thinking
2189. Ask questions! Let your mind wonder, be curious, about things you see. Use those six tiny keys to knowledge again. Ask y_____f what, when, where, how, who, and especially, why!		yourself

2190. Once your curiosity is aroused, you're interested; and when you're in _____d, you'll observe better and with more accuracy.		interested
2191. Learn a bit about things and places you intend to see or visit beforehand. You'll observe more accurately because you'll be able to ask better and more pertinent q_____ns.		questions
2192. A few frames ago I warned you to <u>beware</u> of personal interest. What I mean is that we tend to observe (or even see) what we <u>want</u> to; what we are personally in_____d in.		interested
2193. This can be an asset if you apply the sub-rule of asking questions, and become interested in <u>anything</u> you want to. But, if your attention is <u>only</u> focused on things you are p_____ally interested in, you will be observing or seeing <u>only</u> those things.		personally
2194. This is basic human nature. What we see or hear is usually determined by our own needs, wants, desires and interests. Knowing this, you can make a rule of <u>selective attention.</u> Ask questions about <u>anything;</u> get interested in it, and you're using the rule of s_____ve attention.		selective
2195. We not only see and hear what we·w___t to, but also what we <u>expect</u> to. So beware of personal emotions, loyalties and expectations; they can be-cloud your observation. We tend to see, hear and observe what we want to and what we e_____t to.		want expect
2196. An experiment used to prove this is to flash a card that looks like this : ᏮᏟᏠᏨᏏᏒ, to four different groups of people. Beforehand, each group is told what to e_____t.		expect
2197. One group is told that the word will have something to do with the <u>bad taste of food;</u> the second g___p is told it will be a <u>kind of food;</u> the third is led to believe it will be a <u>clothing accessory</u>, and the fourth group thinks it will have something to do with <u>baseball</u>.		group
2198. ᏮᏟᏠᏨᏏᏒ Upon viewing this half-formed word for a moment, most of the first group will see it as "bitter", a bad t___te of food.		taste

2199. ᚠᛁᛚᛏᛖᚱ Most of the second group will see it as, "butter", a kind of f___d.		food
2200. ᚠᛁᛚᛏᛖᚱ Most of the third group will see it as "button", a cl___ing accessory.		clothing
2201. ᚠᛁᛚᛏᛖᚱ And most of the last group will see it as, "hitter", or "batter", something to do with the game of b_____ll!		baseball
2202. Make up a card with that half-formed word on it, try it on your friends, and you'll see that ɪ is so. People usually see and observe what they ex____ to; or what they're <u>familiar</u> with.		expect
2203. . What we think we see in people, things and actions, is often only an assumption based on want, expectation and habit. I'm referring to the h___t of <u>familiarity</u>.		habit
2204. There is no easy cure for distorted seeing or observing based on interest and familiarity. Part of the battle is to <u>recognize</u> that dis_____ns exist; that we <u>do</u> tend to observe what we want to, expect to, and <u>are</u> familiar with.		distortions
2205. Learn to avoid <u>typing</u> things, people and situations. If you place everything into your own mental 'pigeon holes', you'll be <u>typing</u>; and observing only what you want to and what you e_____t to.		expect

2206. How well you observe accurately is determined by _____ and training.
   a) eyesight
   b) trying
   c) interest
   d) consulting
		c) interest

2207. Let yourself wonder, be curious, about things you see. To do this and become interested, learn to ____
   a) ask questions.
   b) get help.
   c) call friends.
   d) see better.
		a) ask questions.

255

2208. Learn something about things and places you intend to visit be_____nd. Then you'll observe more accurately, because you'll be able to ask better questions.		beforehand

2209. We all tend to see, hear and observe what we _____ to, expect to and what we're familiar with.
    a) ask
    b) give
    c) love
    d) want
		d) want

2210. Use the rule of se_____ve attention. Apply your attention to <u>anything</u> you want to observe, not only the things you are personally interested in.		selective

2211. Beware of the habit of _____ . It can cause distortion in your observation.
    a) indecision.
    b) familiarity.
    c) observation.
    d) association.
		b) familiarity

2212. Don't place people, things and situations into mental pigeon holes. If you do, you're _____ them.
    a) rewarding
    b) insulting
    c) remembering
    d) typing
		d) typing

2213. A while ago, I told you that observation is based on interest and training. I've discussed the interest, now I want to spend a bit of time on the t____ning.		training
2214. It's really just a matter of practice. Police rookies are trained to look for and ob_____ certain tell-tale clues. For example, they know that people who have calluses on their middle fingers, usually do a lot of hand writing.		observe
2215. Finger and palm calluses will usually tell them that the person is, say, a florist or seamstress. Shoulder marks might indicate a mail carrier. Chin and finger marks – a musician. They tr___n themselves; they <u>practice</u> looking for and observing these things.		train
2216. It goes much further, of course. They train themselves to observe characteristic odors of certain professions like, bartenders, butchers, medical personnel, grocers, etc. The rookie must work at, pr_____ce, training his observation.		practice

2217. There are definite ways for <u>you</u> to p_____e observation. The following frames will explain a few of them. First; think of any close friend. Now, with paper and pencil, try to describe his or her face in complete detail.		practice
2218. And I mean, in <u>complete</u> d_____l. Describe the forehead; high, low, bulging, receding, wide, narrow, lined, etc.		detail
2219. Describe the eyes; color, size, protruding, sunken, close-set, wide-set, type of glasses, if any; any peculiarities. D____be the eyebrows; slant up or down, bushy, sparce or normal, plucked, arched, horizontal, connected, heavy, thin, color; ad infinitum.		Describe
2220. Go right down the face in your mind; nose, lips, mouth, teeth, chin, mustache, ears, etc. See if you can describe each part in complete and minute d___l.		detail
2221. The next time you see that friend, check your description. Notice now what you never n_____ed before; or where you were incorrect. Then add those things to your description.		noticed
2222. Try this with other friends. The more you try it the better your ob_____n will become. Try describing the <u>entire</u> person, not just the face. Then, when you become fairly proficient, try looking at a strange face and describing that.		observation
2223. Remember this: the more you look with <u>conscious intention</u> to observe, the more you will observe at each new trial. Ob_____n improves with pr_____ce!		observation practice
2224. All right. Some more ways for you to practice looking with conscious in_____n to observe. Leave the room you're sitting in right now! That's right; leave that room.		intention
2225. Now again, with paper and pencil, try to d_____be that room in complete and minute detail. Position of chairs, ashtrays, lamps. How many pictures, where are they located?		describe

2226. How many windows; size and type of doors; hardware on doors; types of curtains, drapes, shades. Location of telephone, radio, all furniture, etc. List <u>everything</u> you can think of without looking into the r___m.		room
2227. Go into the room and check your list. Notice all the things you <u>didn't</u> list; the things that never <u>registered</u> and were never really ob_____d,		observed.
2228. Now, do it all over again! Your list will grow longer each time you try it. Try the same thing with other r____ms.		rooms
2229. Keep this up for a while, and your sense of ob_____n must improve. This is the finest way I know of actually practicing observation.		observation
2230. Here's another way. Think of a familiar street; one you've walked on many times. See if you can list all the stores on that s_____t! Try listing them in their correct sequence.		street
2231. Then check yourself. Now you'll be looking at that street with con_____s intention to observe. Try it again. The lists will get longer and more accurate as you keep trying it.		conscious
2232. Try looking into a store window for a short time. Then try to list everything displayed there. At first, you'll probably list mostly the items you're personally in_____d in.		interested
2233. But each time you try this, or any of the others, you'll be sharpening your observation. There are many other forms of p_____ce, like trying to identify the year, make and model of passing cars at a glance, as policemen do.		practice
2234. And/or, trying to identify out-of-state license plates by color. Any or all of these practice and training suggestions <u>must</u> sharpen your ob_____n, <u>if you try them.</u>		observation

258

2235. The more you <u>test</u> your observation, the better it will work for you. The more you look and listen with conscious in_____n to observe; with attention and awareness; the sharper, more accurate and more efficient will your ob_____n become.		intention observation
2236. To paraphrase Samuel Johnson; "The true art of o_____n is the art of attention".		observation

2237. The best and probably the only way to train your observation is by consciously _____ observation.
    a) forgetting
    b) remembering
    c) considering
    d) practicing
		d) practicing

2238. Practice observation by making written descriptions of faces, rooms, streets and store windows. Each time you do this the lists will grow l___ger and more accurate.		longer

2239. The more you look at anything with _____ _____ to observe, the more you <u>will</u> observe.
    a) conscious intention
    b) large binoculars
    c) unconscious mind
    d) your eyes
		a) conscious
		   intention

2240. When trying to observe anything in particular, be sure you know exactly what it is you're looking for; be sure the _____ is clear.
    a) idea
    b) observation
    c) attention
    d) goal
		d) goal

2241. All right; observation equals seeing plus _____ .
    a) hearing.
    b) awareness.
    c) touching.
    d) feeling.
		b) awareness.

2242. We see with our eyes but observe with our _____ .
    a) mouths.
    b) intentions.
    c) minds.
    d) attention.
		c) minds.

2243. The main rule for sharpening your sense of observation is to pay _____ .
    a) up.
    b) attention.
    c) more.
    d) bills.
		b) attention.

259

2244. You can learn to pay attention by being
_____.
    a) sick.
    b) disinterested.
    c) bored.
    d) interested.

d) interested.

2245. To 'force' yourself to be interested and
curious, as _____.
    a) questions.
    b) not.
    c) someone.
    d) favors.

a) questions.

2246. When you ask questions about something in
particular and therefore get interested in it, you're
using selective _____.
    a) service.
    b) ideas.
    c) attention.
    d) questions.

c) attention.

2247. Beware of personal interests and expecta-
tions; they can becloud your observations. We
tend to see and hear what we want or _____ .
    a) buy.
    b) expect.
    c) sell.
    d) ridicule.

b) expect.

2248. _____ can cause distortions in your
observation. Beware of it.
    a) Familiarity
    b) Stigmatism
    c) Eyeglasses
    d) Attention

a) Familiarity

2249. The best way to sharpen your sense of observation is to p_____e observation.

practice

2250. The more you look and listen with conscious
_____ to observe, the more you will observe.
    a) mind
    b) conscientiousness
    c) intention
    d) detention

c) intention

2251 But, if I've guided you toward effective
_____ of observation, I've accomplished my purpose.
    a) malpractice
    b) consideration
    c) meaning
    d) practice

d) practice

2252. I can only assure you that in business,
industry or socially, the person who has trained
himself to o_____ will find himself operating
more effectively, more safely and more comfort-
ably than ever before!

observe

260

2253. To sum up this discussion on the art of o_____n; I believe it was Louis Pasteur who said, "Chance favors the prepared mind!" Make sure your mind is prepared to succeed in whatever task you undertake.		observation
YOUR FINAL REVIEW: LET'S SEE HOW MUCH YOUR MENTAL POWERS HAVE GROWN!	No answer required.	
2254. The following frames constitute a complete review of all you've already learned. They are a synopsis; touching on only some of the highlights of the course. The first section dealt with the training of your m____y.		memory
2255. You were taught that a TRAINED MEMORY is based on a_____n. You can re-member a list of items in sequence by associating the previous item to the present item in a ri_____s way. This is the Link system of memory.		association ridiculous
2256. The Peg method taught you to utilize the ph_____c alphabet. The sounds of this alphabet will help you to remember numbers of any kind.		phonetic
2257. In order to remember names and faces you must make up a S_____ W___ for the name and find an outstanding feature on the face.		Substitute Word
2258. If you associate the Substitute Word to the o_____ng feature, you will remember names and faces better than you ever did before.		outstanding
2259. The Substitute Word idea will also aid you in remembering foreign l_____ge vocabulary. Simply make up a Substitute Word for the foreign word and associate it to the English meaning.		language
2260. Use my methods to r_____r lists of items in and out of order, speeches, articles, errands and appointments, addresses, telephone numbers, long-digit numbers, names and faces, foreign language vocabulary, and so on.		remember

2261. To break bad HABITS, apply the 'delay' method. Throw the habit off kilter with the d___ method.		delay
2262. Also the 'time-clock' method. Force yourself to indulge in your bad h____ only at certain times.		habit
2263. The 'coffee break' method has you setting aside certain periods of t___ when you will not indulge in the bad habit.		time
2264. Then there's the 'disturbance' method. Change the usual pattern of your habit by setting up interferences and d_____ces.		disturbances
2265. Make up your mind to avoid the habit for just one full day and you're applying the 'twenty-four ____' method.		hour
2266. Challenge yourself; make mental wagers that you won't indulge in the habit. Try the ch_____ method.		challenge
2267. Finally, try to substitute a good habit for the one you want to break. That's the s_____n method.		substitution
2268. The key to acquiring good habits is attention. Do anything with conscious att_____ often enough and it must become habit.		attention
2269. Define the habit you wish to form, in detail. Make a voiced or written pledge. Then practice the action at the proper times only and in a definite way. Do it consistently and it will become a h____.		habit

262

2270. The first rule for strengthening your WILL POWER is: Be sure you want it badly e___gh.		enough
2271. The second rule for strengthening your will power is: Have _____ that you can do it. a) proof b) hopes c) confidence d) desires		c) confidence
2272. The most important rule is simply to _____ . a) forget. b) begin. c) remember. d) drop it.		b) begin
2273. The fourth rule is: Back yourself into a c_____ occasionally.		corner
2274. The final rule for strengthening your will power is: Form the h___t.		habit
2275. Some of the main rules for controlling WORRY AND FEAR are: Make yourself realize that most of the things you _____ about seldom happen.		worry
2276. Learn to accept the inevitable. For minor worries and frustration, it will help to anticipate, overcome and accept the in_____ .		inevitable
2277. One of the best ways to control chronic worrying is to prepare for the worst that can happen. Once you've p_____d for the worst, there's no longer any need to worry.		prepared
2278. Do something about the thing that's worrying you; and try to belittle its importance. Minimize its effect on you by ridiculing and be_____ing it.		belittling

2279. Another tip is to think of all the reasons you can why a particular stress or worry should <u>not</u> exist or bother you. Learn to r _____ your worry.
    a) remember
    b) recite   (see next frame)
	Your answer should go below ↓	

2279. (continued)
 	
    c) realize
    d) rationalize
		d) rationalize

2280. Finally, try to make up your mind that you will do all your w____ing on one special day of each week.		worrying
2281. The most important rule for controlling and conquering irrational fear, is to <u>do</u> the thing you ____ .		fear
2282. A good tip is to pretend or act as if your ____ of any particular thing or situation simply didn't exist.		fear
2283. It is helpful to confide your fears to someone you trust. Don't bottle up your f___s and w____s.		fears worries
2284. Stop being afraid or worried about the future. Take care of the p____t and the future will usually take care of itself.		present
2285. In order to GET PEOPLE TO DO WHAT YOU WANT, you have to make <u>them</u> want it. Find out what <u>they</u> really want, then demonstrate how what <u>you</u> w___ will help them get it. Get <u>your</u> g__l working in him.		want goal
2286. Learn to show appreciation. The desire to be a_____ed is the deepest feeling or desire of human nature.		appreciated

2287. Help people to save face if you possibly can. Above all, consider the other person's pride. Consider his pride and help him save ___ .		face
2288. Handling p___le boils down to recognizing the underlying principle of self-interest and the center-of-the-world feeling which is deeply imbedded in all of us.		people
2289. The four main rules to help you THINK CREATIVELY are: First: locate or z___ in on a need.		zero
2290. Second; find the simple _____ mainly by asking questions. a) solution b) problem c) location d) illustration		a) solution
2291. The third rule for idea creating is: Let your _____ go to work. a) hands b) subconscious c) feet d) friends		b) subconscious
2292. Finally, ask questions and try to sell yourself on your idea. The rule is: Put it to the t__t.		test
2293. CONCENTRATION is exclusive attention to any one object or subject. The Golden Rule for applying ex_____ att_____; to concentrate; is - get yourself involved.		exclusive attention
2294. The best way to get yourself involved is to ask q_____s.		questions
2295. When you read, keep in mind that you are looking for specific a_____s to specific questions.		answers

	Your answer should go below ↓	
2296. As you read you will know it when a sentence answers one of your questions. When it does, slow down and read that sentence carefully. Then, most important, _____ that sentence. a) underline b) forget (see next frame)		
2296. (continued) c) paraphrase d) consider		a) underline
2297. Follow the rules and you'll learn to c _____te as you read. You're involved and giving your exclusive attention to the reading matter.		concentrate
2298. The human brain thinks about four times as fast as the tongue can speak. This gap provides the time for mind-wandering as you try to listen. Fill those time gaps by getting yourself in_____d.		involved
2299. Ask yourself questions. <u>Summarize</u> what the speaker has said. <u>Anticipate</u> his next point. L___n between the lines and ask yourself if you <u>agree</u> with the speaker.		Listen
2300. Ask these questions while listening to speeches, lectures or conversations, and you'll eliminate mind-w_____ing; you'll be able to <u>maintain attention.</u>		wandering
2301. Asking questions is also the first rule for problem-s_____g.		solving
2302. The second rule for PROBLEM-SOLVING is: Define your p_____m precisely.		problem
2303. The third rule is an obvious one: Get the facts. The necessary tools for any type of thinking, are f___s.		facts

2304. The fourth rule is: Keep an open mind and weigh all factors of the _____m.		problem
2305. Finally, let your thought lead to action. After gathering all the facts and going through the self-questioning, come to a decision and go into a____n.		action
2306. Effective reading, rapid reading and RAPID LEARNING all go hand in hand. Effective r___ing is a search for ideas, thoughts and answers.		reading
2307. The three main rules for effective reading are: One; locate the main thoughts in the mass of w__ds that contain them.		words
2308. Two: spear or separate each thought you've l___ted.		located
2309. And three; boil each located and sep_____d thought or idea down to a few easily remembered words.		separated
2310. Build a 'road map' of any book by using the 'big' signposts of the title, table of c_____ts, index and preface or foreword. Then utilize the individual chapter s_____ts.		contents signposts

2311. Do so and you're applying the technique of pre-_____.
    a) tending.
    b) paying.
    c) reading.
    d) listening.
		c) reading

2312. One rule for helping to ORGANIZE TIME is to form the habit of deciding about the little things in___ly.		instantly

2313. Another rule is to make a p___ for each day; then commit yourself to it.		plan
2314. Learn to concentrate on doing one thing at a time. F___sh one Job or chore before going on to the next one.		Finish
2315. Except when faced with tasks that really worry you, do the things that <u>can</u> wait first, then get the ur___t ones off your mind.		urgent

2316. A good rule to try to follow is: Handle any correspondence or paper ____ ___.
     a) only alone.
     b) only twice.
     c) only once.
     d) only carefully.
		c) only once

2317. Learn to make routine and repetitive chores automatic and h____ual. And always try to start things on t___.		habitual time
2318. When making your plan for the day, leave a 'c_____n' of time for each duty or chore.		'cushion'
2319. The first, and really the only, rule for sharpening your POWERS OF OBSERVATION is: P___ a_____n.		Pay attention
2320. This is done by cultivating your interest and curiosity. Since we observe what we're in _____d in, use selective attention to become interested in anything you want to.		interested
2321. Look at things with f___sed attention and they'll register on your mind. They'll be observed.		focused

268

2322. The best way to train your observation is to pr___ce it.		practice
2323. The more you look or listen with <u>conscious</u> <u>intention</u> to _____ , the more you <u>will</u> observe.		observe
2324. Well, you've just finished this PROGRAMED LEARNING course. You've finished reading it and answering the questions, but you should <u>never</u> f___h applying the things you've learned.		finish
2325. You're well on your way toward an organized mind. And, if I've taught you only that it is training and org_____n of the mind which alone can lead you toward a happy and successful life, I've more than accomplished what I set out to do.		organization
2326. If you make up your mind, if you <u>resolve</u>, to <u>use</u> the ideas, rules, techniques and suggestions herein contained, they cannot help but aid you in your b_____ss, social and everyday life.		business
2327. So for the last time, let me stress again the imp_____ce of applying, <u>using</u> and <u>trying</u> all the hints and rules I've given you. Get actively involved instead of just passively reading.		importance
2328. May I leave you with one thought – "There is nothing either good or bad, but thinking makes it so." --Shakespeare	↑ ↑	
	↑ ↑	
	↑ ↑	

CONGRATULATIONS! — You have now concluded Harry Lorayne's INSTANT MIND POWER course!

If you've done everything as you were instructed, you've undoubtedly already felt the improvement in your ability to use the remarkable power which was locked up inside your own mind. And as you put these principles to continued use, your continual improvement will astound you, your friends, and your associates.

Keep this course as you would an especially valuable book and review all that you've learned from time to time. Thus it will provide a periodic refresher course in INSTANT MIND POWER.